SHIPWRECKS
From the Tees to the Tyne

SHIPWRECKS
From the Tees to the Tyne

Maureen Anderson

Wharncliffe Books

First Published in 2007 by
Wharncliffe Books
an imprint of
Pen and Sword Books Limited
47 Church Street, Barnsley, South Yorkshire S70 2AS

For up-to-date information on other titles produced under the
Wharncliffe imprint, please telephone or write to:

Wharncliffe Books
FREEPOST
47 Church Street
Barnsley
South Yorkshire S70 2BR
Telephone (24 hours): 01226 734555

ISBN: 1 84563 020 3

Printed and bound in England
by Biddles Ltd

Pen & Sword Books Ltd incorporates the Imprints of:
Pen & Sword Aviation, Pen & Sword Maritime, Pen & Sword Military,
Wharncliffe Books, Pen & Sword Select,
Pen & Sword Military Classics and Leo Cooper

For a complete list of Pen & Sword titles please contact:
PEN & SWORD BOOKS LIMITED
47 Church Street, Barnsley, South Yorkshire, S70 2AS, England
E-mail: enquiries@pen-and-sword.co.uk
Website: www.pen-and-sword.co.uk

Contents

Introduction and Acknowledgements 6

PART I *Seaton Carew, Hartlepool and Blackhall* 13

  1 The Hartlepool Fishermen, 1815 21

  2 The Longscar Rocks, 1830 .22

  3 The Strange Case of the *Amelia*, 1840 24

  4 A Fatal Decision, 1852 24

  5 Hartlepool Heugh, 1854 25

  6 New Year But No Respite 26

  7 Blackhall Rocks, 1860 29

  8 The Great Storm, 1861 31

  9 The Compass Box, 1865 35

 10 An Accusation of Neglect, 1866 36

 11 The Tragedy of the *Francais*, 1874 37

 12 Hartlepool Bay, 1880 40

 13 A Dramatic Rescue, 1883 42

 14 The Loss of the *Granite*, 1888 44

 15 The *Dauntless* and the *Trio*, 1901 45

 16 The Last Voyage of the SS *Clavering*, 1907 51

 17 The Coastguard and the Villagers, 1912 59

 18 The Last Masted Sailing Ship, 1930 63

 19 Gallantry Medals 67

PART II *Seaham and Sunderland* 71

 20 Fire on Deck, 1794 75

 21 The Monkwearmouth Pilots, 1852 76

 22 A Catalogue of Catastrophies, 1854 77

23 The Sunderland Piers, 1857 79

24 Disaster for a Fleet, 1861 81

25 A Cliff Rescue, 1874 83

26 Breeches Buoy, 1880 84

27 The Fate of the *Aurora*, 1885 86

28 A New Century, 1901 89

29 Gallantry Medals 92

PART III *Shields, Tynemouth and Cullercoats* 93

30 A Disgraceful Scene, 1852 99

31 Nine on the Rocks, 1853-4 101

32 The Herd Sand, 1857 103

33 The *Lovely Nelly*, 1861 104

34 The *Stanley* and the *Friendship*, 1864 111

35 The *Earl Percy* and others, 1865 115

36 Volunteer Life Brigades 117

37 Storm Times Two, 1876 120

38 A Heavy Toll, 1880 123

39 A Busy Watch, 1882 124

40 More Casualties, 1901 125

41 Gallantry Medals 128

Conclusion 131

Sources 140

Glossary 141

Index 142

Dedication

For my mother, Margaret Joyce Anderson, 1916-96, who spent her early years in Tynemouth watching the pier sparkle in the summer sun, and disappear under the breakers during the winter storms. After many years of travelling, she returned to live out her twilight years in Cullercoats, near to the sea she loved so much. Her respect for the ever changing moods of the North Sea led her to become an ardent supporter of, and a beneficiary to, the RNLI. Her memory, and that of others like her, lives on in the lifeboat that at present serves the Tynemouth area of the coast. She was a true *Northumberland Spirit*.

Also for the past, present and future rescuers of those in peril from shipwreck, and for the thousands of seafarers who were lost in, and those that were saved from, the fickle North Sea.

Introduction

A storm arises, forcing its waters in mighty billows, which course each other towards the point, raging and dashing as if the rocks were about to be torn up from their very foundations. What form do I perceive through the thickening darkness by the aid of the flashing fire? Surely it is an embayed ship, full of human beings at the mercy of the elements. Her rudder gone, she drives directly down upon those terrible rocks: there is no port no harbour of refuge for her; she must inevitably be dashed to pieces as she nears the point. See, she throws out signals of distress! They are seen and answered by the Holy Brotherhood, and all are in motion to assist. Some of them fly to the hardy fishermen, whose hovels may be seen without the convent walls: but these men, bold as they are, have no vessel capable of braving such a storm, or living in such a sea. No boat of life is there, and death is inevitable to all on board. Hear the booming of the convent bell, in the fearful lull of the storm; and see, a fire is rising upon the point to indicate to the hapless beings on board that their struggles for life, although they cannot be assisted, are observed and cared for – they at least have sympathy.

A procession of the brotherhood, with some of the sacred utensils of the altar headed by the emblem of their salvation raised high in the air, place themselves on the most exposed point, and ever and anon, above the roaring tempest, may be heard the solemn service of the church, as it fervently rises from the kneeling, supplicating throng.

As the ship is driven nearer, on board can be seen a stout, strong man, striving to do what remains to him of duty. Now he holds by the mast, and looks on, with calmness on his face, as if conscious he had weathered as fierce a storm as this before, and yet escaped. But lo! A mighty wave has lifted the vessel on its crest, and in descending, she strikes the rock: her masts are gone; the deck is swept by the rolling flood, and all is engulfed in the boiling, raging waters. The strong man has seized a spar and bears himself bravely, raising his head, and shaking the water from his shaggy hair.

A female appears on the wreck that bears in one arm a helpless child, whilst with the other, she closely clings to the once gallant bark. The strong man sees this, and using his utmost efforts to near the wreck, the woman leaps into the water towards him, in the agony of despair. He springs with all his strength, but misses his aim, securing only the child, whilst the mother is whirled far from him on the billows. He now has an additional motive to struggle for life: and holding the child with one strong arm, firmly grasps the spar with the other.

The waves come on with maddening roll, until one, more gigantic than the rest, overwhelms him and his burden: he rises to the surface, but alas! The child is gone; and then for the first time, tears fill his eyes as he directs them towards the cliff.

At this instant the cross is raised on high; he hears the toll of the bell, and the sound of voices pleading in his behalf. With one more convulsive effort he raises his clasped hands, directing his gaze to the holy group; but a vast wave strikes him down, and he is buried in the mighty ocean, till he hears the Almighty voice call to the sea to give up its dead.

This extract, from a small booklet, *The Bay of Hartlepool*, written in 1856 by the renowned geologist, William Hutton, for Charles Ward Jackson, son of the founder of West Hartlepool, paints a vivid picture of the helplessness of man against the violence of the elements of nature and the unpredictable North Sea. Up and down the North East coast the graveyards accommodate many an unnamed, drowned seafarer. Families in far away places would wait in vain for their loved ones to return from a sea voyage.

The North East coast is made up of diversifying scenery with long sandy beaches, rocky outcrops, shale covered inlets and high rugged cliffs. Looking along the coastline and out to the North Sea in mild weather the whole forms a stunning panorama. In inclement weather the scene can change in an instant. Fierce storms bring sleet, snow and rain so there is little or no visibility. The wind churns the sea until it rages and boils over and around any vessel that happens to be unlucky enough to be caught in its grasp. The crews of the early sailing ships relied partially on the wind to carry them to their chosen destinations but, too often, it carried them to their deaths. The loss of a crew, not only caused untold grief, but could leave a large family without a breadwinner. Many mothers would have lost their sons as it was common for the early vessels to carry young boys as apprentices or cabin boys. All too often, if a vessel was caught in high seas, these children would be the first to be washed overboard, probably because of a lack of strength to keep their grip against the force of the waves. The loss of ships and their cargoes did not affect only those directly concerned with the crew or the vessel. It affected every human being in one way or another. Commodities that were not available in one country or area were brought by sea from another. If cargo was continuously lost those items would become harder to obtain and, of course, this would push prices up.

The earliest recorded rescues were carried out by fishermen launching their own small boats and rowing as near to the stricken vessels as possible. The sailors would often jump from their ship into the freezing waters in the hope that they could be pulled onto the small rescue boat before they were swept away or overcome by the numbing cold and drowned. By the end of the eighteenth and beginning of the nineteenth century boats were being built to specific designs with the saving of life in mind. The earliest surviving lifeboat in Britain is the *Zetland*, built by Henry Greathead in 1802, which is on display at the Redcar Lifeboat Museum. This, and other early lifeboats used in the north, were known as 'North Country' boats. The boat was mounted on a carriage which would then be pulled to the launching site by a team of horses, usually up to eight in number, with the four front horses and riders entering the water. There would also be a team of helpers to assist in getting the boat over the sand and into the water. The crew would number between thirteen and twenty, depending on the size of boat. By the middle of the nineteenth century lifeboat design had improved and self-righting boats were in use.

The lifeboat would carry ropes attached to large hooks or grapnels. These would be thrown onto the ship and used as a means of forming a direct line between it and the lifeboat. The rope could then be used to bring the lifeboat closer alongside and to aid the seamen to reach the lifeboat.

In certain circumstances, where a lifeboat would not be able to reach a stricken vessel, perhaps on a rocky outcrop near the coast where the water was too shallow or a great distance from a lifeboat station, a rocket firing line would be used. A line would be fired at a ship and, once the endangered crew had managed to take hold of it, they would haul a block and pulley to their vessel. This contraption, once secured, would form an endless rope between the vessel and the rescuers. By this means a small boat could be hauled through the surf or a type of basket, known as a breeches buoy, sent to the vessel to transport the crew and passengers to the shore. This was made of a canvas cradle attached to a cork float. The cradle had two holes in the base through which the occupier put his or her legs. If the cradle went into the water the cork float would keep the occupant's head above water and prevent him or her from drowning. The rocket lines could also be used by tugs, usually at high tide, to try and pull a ship from where it was stranded.

The earliest of this type of apparatus was Captain Manby's rocket which was fired using mortar and shell. Then, in about 1825, John Dennett was marketing a rocket to be used as a military weapon from ships. He altered the design, making it portable, so that the equipment could be carried by two or three men to wherever it was needed and used for rescues from a rocky beach or a cliff. There was also Boxer's rocket in use. These all eventually gave way to the improved design of Carte's rocket, which was widely used in Britain. There were problems associated with the rocket lines. One was the force and direction of the wind. It was sometimes impossible to make a direct hit on to the distressed vessel because the wind would carry the line off course. The other was that if too much force was used or the line was old and weak it would break.

By the end of the nineteenth century masted sailing vessels were fast becoming a thing of the past as ships powered by steam took over the seas. However, there were still many catastrophes, especially near the coast. Although steam ships did not rely on the wind being behind them for their movement the pilots could not see through fog and it was not until the invention of radar in the 1940s that they were able to navigate to avoid obstacles, such as hidden rock formations, sandbanks and other ships.

In the early years of the lifeboat stations, the coxswain would be paid a small sum annually for his services to the lifeboat. In Hartlepool and Seaton Carew this was recorded as being one guinea. For every rescue or attempted rescue, he and his crew would receive a reward depending on the circumstances. Helpers and the owners of the horses that were used would also receive a payment for their assistance. These sums were funded from subscriptions and donations.

In past times it was commonplace for fathers, sons, brothers and other male members of a family to follow in the same trade or skill. The lifeboat crews were no exception and there could be up to six members of three generations of the same family assisting at a rescue. Tracing our ancestors has become the passion of many in recent years so, wherever possible, I have included the names of those involved in the events related in these chapters.

Within these pages joy and sorrow walk hand in hand with tales of heroism and tragedy. There have been many thousands of wrecks and rescues, both recorded and unrecorded. These are the stories of just a few of the severe storms, shipwrecks and rescues, courage and despair that took place along the North East coast at the mouth of the Tees, Seaton Carew, Hartlepool, Blackhall, Seaham, Sunderland, Shields, Tynemouth and Cullercoats up to the twentieth century.

Acknowledgements

Alf Carney, George Colley, George Nairn, Bill and Francis Cox and Myra Docherty for information on and the use of images. Alistair Peacock for his assistance regarding the history of the Hood family. The staff of Hartlepool Reference Library for, as always, their courteous assistance in answering queries and searching for relevant information. A special thank you to Gary Green of Tees Archaeology and Charlotte Taylor of Hartlepool Arts and Museums for their patience and valuable assistance. Thanks are also due to Mrs M Sherris, Francis Cox and Myra Docherty. Brian Elliott, Commissioning Editor at Wharncliffe Books, for his continuous advice and support. Last but not least my husband, Jim, always with me every step of the way.

Part I

Seaton Carew,
Hartlepool and Blackhall

*B*efore the breakwaters were built there was nothing to halt the fury of the sea from Hartlepool to Redcar during a storm. The vulnerable sailing ships would be tossed about like matchsticks and thrown against the sandbanks, cliffs, rocks or shore with the total loss of vessels and lives over the centuries unrecorded. Hartlepool had been an important port from the twelfth to the sixteenth century when it had been used for import by the Bishops of Durham. The port then went into decline with the small population of 1,000 or so relying mainly on fishing for their livelihood. By the end of the eighteenth century there was a huge demand for coal. In major reclamation feats, beginning in 1810, the course of the Tees was altered by straightening bends and removing sandbanks to make navigation of the river easier and safer for shipping.

A postcard depicting the mouth of the Tees with the South Gare lighthouse in the distance. Author's collection

The Hartlepool Heugh in rough weather. Author's collection

Hartlepool was in an ideal position to accommodate sailing vessels without them having to use the river, but major construction work was required for it to become an influential port once more.

The Hartlepool Harbour and Middleton pier were opened in 1835 and Victoria Dock in 1840. The South Gare was under construction from 1863-88 and the North Gare from 1882-91. These were constructed using the waste slag from the ironworks in the area, which the ironmasters were only too happy to be rid of and even delivered free of charge. By the time the North Gare was completed steam ships, which could manoeuvre against the wind, were taking over from the masted sailing vessels.

In August 1802 a meeting took place at the Castle Eden inn with the purpose of funding and providing a lifeboat for Hartlepool. By February 1803 the first lifeboat was in place in a boathouse recorded as adjoining the Watergate which probably referred to the Sandwell Gate, so this boathouse would have been sited on the Fish Sands. By 1855 there were three lifeboat stations at Hartlepool. In January 1875 the management of the stations was taken over by the RNLI.

There appear to be no surviving records as to the names or donors of the very early lifeboats at Hartlepool. The names that were recorded up until the twentieth century consisted of:

James Davidson Shaw, a legacy of JD Shaw of Newcastle in 1847.
Foresters Pride, a gift of the Ancient Order of Foresters in 1869 and
another boat of the same name and by the same donor in 1887.
Rochdale, a gift of the Rochdale Lifeboat Fund in 1879 and
another boat of the same name and from the same donor in 1887.
Charles Mather, a gift of Mrs Jerningham of Berwick-on-Tweed in
1876.
Ilminster, a gift of George Lovibond of Ilminster in 1889.
Charles Ingleby, from the trust fund of Rev Charles Ingleby of
Birmingham in 1876 and another boat of the same name and from
the same legacy in 1887.
John Clay Barlow, gift of Miss Sarah Barlow of Leicester in 1879.
Cyclist, gift of the Cyclists Jubilee Fund in 1887.

There have been many devastating storms on the North East coast
throughout the centuries and, perhaps not the worst, but certainly the
most memorable for the town of Hartlepool was in 1861. This became
known as the Great Storm. One reason this particular storm has gone
down in the annals of local maritime history was because it was
daylight when most of the ships were wrecked and the havoc wreaked
on ships and men was witnessed by hundreds of people watching
helplessly from the shores. Another reason was the controversy that
had been going on in Hartlepool for some time concerning a Harbour
of Refuge. Everyone who had any interest in the port of the town, and
that was the larger proportion of the population, knew how dangerous
the seas around Hartlepool were to shipping. For many years the
influential business men of the town had campaigned for a Harbour of
Refuge but it was never built because money could not be found to
finance such an expensive scheme. If this harbour had been in place
during the Great Storm many of the lives, cargo and ships would not
have been lost. It would have also given Hartlepool a reputation as
being a safe harbour and this would have brought an enormous
amount of trade to the area which may have more than compensated
for the expense of the construction.

In 1851, building began on the Hartlepool Heugh, a breakwater
jutting out from the Headland to make it safer for shipping to get into
the port, but the work was halted after the erection of 750 feet (229m)
in case it upset the plans for the Harbour of Refuge. Eventually, in
1870, the Heugh was completed to a length of 600 feet (183m).

From the eighteenth century wealthy Quakers travelled from
Sunderland and Darlington to spend their summer leisure time in
Seaton Carew believing that the sea air was salubrious. Many of them
became benefactors to the village by giving large donations towards
buildings, education and other commodities that benefited the entire

The Jesse Stevens *was sailing from Newcastle to London on when she became stranded at Teesmouth on Saturday, 14 April 1849. This artist's impression was sketched when the Seaton Carew lifeboat the* Tees *was launched to go to the aid of the crew who were saved with great difficulty. There is no record as to whether or not the vessel was a total loss. The* Tees *was in service from 1824-57 and was instrumental in saving 188 lives.* Author's collection

population of the village. One such benefactor was Thomas Backhouse, from Darlington, but with family connections in Sunderland. In September 1823 he was standing on the beach with William Hood, a Seaton pilot. They watched helplessly as a ship went to pieces on the Longscar Rocks and the cries of the doomed crew reached their ears above the storm. According to a newspaper report of the time and the story passed down through the Hood family from father to son, Thomas had turned to William, saying: 'Dost thou think that if thou had a lifeboat thou could have saved that crew?' Will's answer was: 'Aye Sir, every soul.' Thomas replied: 'Then thou shall have a lifeboat.' Shortly afterwards a lifeboat was sent to Seaton from Sunderland and placed in the charge of William Hood. Thomas was born in 1750 so would have been about seventy-three at this time. He died early in 1824, it was said, at the same time his lifeboat, *Tees*, was performing its first rescue. A small publication issued by the Ladies Auxiliary in c.1896 states that, during its thirty-four years of service, 188 lives were saved by this lifeboat. William Hood was the coxswain for thirty of those years until his son, Robert, took over to be followed later by another of his sons, Henry. That the *Tees* was built in

Sunderland is fairly certain but the name of the builder is not recorded. This first boat must have been of extremely sturdy construction as, although it is not known where she spent the intervening years, a record shows that she was sold in 1877, twenty years after her retirement as a lifeboat, for £15, possibly for firewood. The money was used to build a wall to keep grazing cattle away from the boathouse.

At a meeting held in the Stockton Town Hall in January 1825, a subscription was entered into for the purpose of forming a fund to promote the Preservation of Life in Cases of Shipwreck, and the Society of that name was formed. This would have been the beginnings of what was to become the Tees Bay Lifeboat and Shipwreck Society.

The first RNLI Seaton Carew lifeboat, Charlotte, *outside the lifeboat house at South End, Seaton Carew, c1857. There were two lifeboats of this name, one from 1857-67 and the second from 1867-73. Between them they were instrumental in saving sixty-five lives.* Author's collection

When the Seaton Carew Lifeboat Branch was formed there were not enough men in the village to man the boat. In the event of the lifeboat being required to be launched to perform a service to a distressed vessel, a flag would be raised to alert the Hartlepool fishermen, who would then promptly come to Seaton Carew to make up the numbers needed.

The lifeboat Francis Whitbourn *which gave service from 1908 until 1922 when the Seaton Carew Lifeboat Station closed. This lifeboat was instrumental in saving twenty-one lives.* Hartlepool Arts and Museums

The Francis Whitbourn *in her boathouse with her crew which consisted of coxswain John Franklin, William Franklin, James and John Lithgo, Harry and John Bulmer, James and Albert Anderson, Thomas Storer, John Cuthbertson, Thomas Harrison, George Hodgson and Thomas Cooke.* Hartlepool Arts and Museums

The Bradford, *a motor lifeboat that was stationed on the Seaton Snook in 1907.*

Throughout almost a century of its history the Seaton Carew Station had eight lifeboats. The replacement for the *Tees* in 1857 was the first RNLI lifeboat, *Charlotte*, donated by William McKerrell of Argyle and named after his wife. A second *Charlotte*, from the same donor, was in service from 1867-73. This was followed by the *Job Hindley*, donated by Job Hindley of Manchester, who made his money from tripe dressing. In 1888 a new boat that was unnamed was provided by the RNLI. The Seaton villagers wanted the boat named after their beloved vicar and Honorary Secretary to the Seaton Carew Lifeboat Branch but the RNLI insisted that the new boat was to be the *Mary Isabella*, after its Manchester donor. After much argument, even leading to the resignation of the Seaton Local Committee and the lifeboat crew refusing to take the new boat out to sea, the *Mary Isabella* was sent to Ramsey Lifeboat Station. Another boat was supplied unnamed and, to the villager's delight, they were able to christen her the *John Lawson*. In 1906 the *Charles Ingleby* was borrowed from Hartlepool on a temporary basis. The *Bradford*, a motor lifeboat, was placed at the Snook in 1907 but was found not to be cost effective as a caretaker had to be employed to watch that she was not vandalised or stolen. The *Bradford* was removed after a short time to Seaham and was returned to the area in 1911 to become the first lifeboat at the Teesmouth Lifeboat Station. The last lifeboat, *Francis Whitbourn*, was donated in 1908 by Robert Lodge. The station was taken over by the RNLI at the request of the Honorary Secretary, Reverend John Lawson, in 1857. It closed in 1922 partly because of a lack of labour to man the boat, all the old salts had either moved away or died, and partly because it was decided that any further rescues could be dealt with by the Hartlepool, Redcar and Teesmouth Stations.

1. The Hartlepool Fishermen, 1815

On Saturday 28 January 1815, with a tremendous gale blowing, Captain William Evans of Monkwearmouth and his crew of eight were on the heavily laden *Betsy* when she struck ground less than a mile from shore near Seaton Carew. Those watching from the beach immediately alerted the Hartlepool fishermen. Within the hour the lifeboat had been brought from Hartlepool to Seaton Carew and was launched with a crew of seventeen. Those observing from the shore held their breath and gasped in turn as the drama unfolded. Huge waves washed over the lifeboat as the crew put all their strength into manning the oars. The cries of the men aboard the doomed ship could be heard even above the howling wind and this spurred the lifeboat crew to even greater effort. Eventually they were alongside the *Betsy* whose hull was now under water. As the sailors jumped from the rigging to reach the lifeboat, three missed their aim and fell into the water but were quickly seized and dragged to safety. With eight of the sailors aboard, the lifeboat made its way to shore amidst the clapping and cheering of the spectators, but one poor man had been left behind on the *Betsy* clinging desperately to the rigging. Some of the lifeboat crew were so exhausted and benumbed by the cold that their strength was gone, so the lifeboat was launched once more with twelve of the crew replaced by fresh hands. The last man was plucked to safety from the bowsprit just as the *Betsy* went to pieces and was completely wrecked. The rescued and the rescuers were led to the Seaton Hotel where the landlady, Mrs Galbraith, saw to their refreshment and every need.

The two lifeboat crews consisted of:

First Launch	Second Launch
Anthony Pounder, pilot ruler	Anthony Pounder *
Thomas Watt, pilot	Thomas Watt *
John Horsley, pilot	John Horsley *
James Harrison, fisherman	James Harrison *
Robert Hodgson, sailor	Robert Hodgson *
John Davison, pilot	Thomas Coulson, pilot
John Pounder, pilot	J Cambridge, boat builder
Matthew Hunter, pilot	John Kennedy, fisherman
George Horsley, pilot	Robert Snowdon, fisherman
John Shepherd, pilot	Francis Boagey, fisherman
Robert Harrison, sailor	John Boagey, fisherman
W Huntridge, fisherman	James Coulson, fisherman
James Pounder, fisherman	Thomas Hood, fisherman
Thomas Pounder, fisherman	Josh Hastings, fisherman
John Leeming, fisherman	John Shepherd, fisherman
Francis Hastings, fisherman	Robert Hunter, fisherman
Thomas Robson, fisherman	William Horsley

* *went out twice*

Shortly afterwards a letter was received by Sir Cuthbert Sharp, the Secretary of the Lifeboat Committee which read as follows:

Sunderland, February 8th 1815
Honoured Sir, This comes with our kind thanks for having saved our lives on the 28th of last month; crew, consisting of nine in number, were snatched from death by the Hartlepool Lifeboat, and as long as we live we shall ever pray for and return thanks to the Hartlepool fishermen.

The letter was signed by Captain William Evans, mate William Douglas and the crew: William Cole, John Trew, John Williamson, John Scott, Alexander Jackson, William Wilkinson and James Price.

<hr />

2. The Longscar Rocks, 1830

On Tuesday, 12 December 1830 a severe gale began to rage with the wind blowing NNE. Before the storm completed venting its fury it was to claim many lives. The first reported tragedy was a coal-laden sloop, *Newcastle*, which was seen being driven by wind and the huge waves onto the Longscar Rocks. The state of the tide caused a long delay in the launch of the Hartlepool lifeboat and by the time she was underway it was too late to be of any assistance. The lifeboat *Tees* was launched from a little to the north of Carr House with Coxswain William Hood and a crew made up of both Hartlepool and Seaton Carew men. The crew of the sloop could be seen clinging to the rigging but the lifeboat men's strenuous efforts to reach the stricken vessel in time were in vain. Before they could get near enough to assist, the sloop went bottom up and Captain Crowder along with all his crew was lost.

On Thursday morning of the same week an eyewitness stood near Cliff House at Seaton Carew and saw a tragedy unfold. That afternoon he wrote a letter describing the heart-rending events that took place. The writer was William Vollum, Chairman of the Society for the Preservation of Life in Cases of Shipwreck and the recipient of the letter was Mr T Randyll, the treasurer of the same society.

A team of eight horses and riders lined up on Seaton beach ready for lifeboat practice. Hartlepool Arts and Museums

On Thursday, 3 August 1900, during severe gales the William Crowe, *a brigantine built in 1841, was sailing from Yarmouth to Hartlepool in ballast. Early in the afternoon she was seen to be in trouble. The crew could not negotiate the harbour because of the driving rain. The Hartlepool No 2 lifeboat was launched under the supervision of the Coxswain, Richard Robinson. Captain John Lake and his crew of four were taken off the vessel with great difficulty. The crew were all over the age of sixty and were utterly exhausted by their efforts. The* William Crowe *was eventually carried by the breakers onto Stranton beach and, although her masts were still more or less intact, she had received such a buffeting that she became a total wreck.* Hartlepool Arts and Museums

Vollum wrote that he had watched as a brig was driven onto the Longscar Rocks. Without delay the lifeboat *Tees* was launched with Coxswain William Hood and his crew making every effort to reach the stricken ship. They struggled for a considerable time with the huge waves driving them back again and again. As the brig began to go to pieces the lifeboat manoeuvred around the large pieces of floating wreckage as they frantically searched for signs of life in the freezing waters. A man was spotted and the boat was quickly at his side. Some of the crew grasped his jacket and shirt but his clothes came away in their hands as they tried to disentangle him from the wreckage of ropes and rigging; and, not being able to free him, he had to be left to his fate. Eventually, they managed to drag two other men from the turbulent waters to safety.

Vollum later learned that the brig was the *Marchioness* (or *Marquis*) *of Huntley*, owned by Messrs Martin & Co of Stockton. She traded between Stockton and Newcastle and had been fully laden with coal when she went down. Out of the crew of nine, only the master and carpenter were rescued.

3. The Strange Case of the *Amelia*, 1840

On a chill winter afternoon in 1840, with strong ENE winds blowing and the mouth of the Tees a mass of churning broken water, two vessels were seen running before the wind trying to reach safe harbour. One, a London vessel, called *Amelia*, had lost all her sails and was heading dangerously close to the Longscar Rocks. The Seaton Carew villagers who were watching from shore sent a summons to William Hood, the coxswain of the lifeboat, that his services were required. The *Tees* was taken along the beach, manned with local pilots and fishermen and launched. As the lifeboat approached the *Amelia* a huge wave engulfed her and she was rolled over. When the spray cleared neither a mast nor a living soul could be seen on her deck and the vessel pitched and rolled at the mercy of the sea. The lifeboat crew searched through the bobbing pieces of wreckage and, getting as near as they could to the vessel, shouted to see if anyone had survived. There was no reply so it was assumed her crew were lost and the lifeboat was returned to the shore. The *Tees* was put back in her boathouse and the men went with heavy hearts to their homes. As the Hood family were talking over the day's events one of William's sons, Robert, who would have been about eighteen at that time, said that he had a strong feeling that there might still be men alive on the *Amelia* and that they may have been below deck to protect themselves from the wash of the sea. William must have trusted his son's judgement because he called the crew out of their warm homes to re-launch the lifeboat. With some difficulty this was achieved and the crew headed out to the site of the wreck. As they approached the vessel cries for help were heard and the lifeboat crew's spirits soared. It took a tremendous effort but, with the aid of a rope, six surviving members of an original crew of twelve were taken onto the lifeboat from the rapidly disintegrating vessel. They were just about to cast off the line and row for shore when they were told there was still one man left behind, alive, but with a broken leg and unable to move. Robert pulled himself onto the pitching vessel and, within a short time was on the deck with the crippled seaman on his back. Willing hands helped them onto to the lifeboat and the seven survivors were taken safely to solid ground.

4. A Fatal Decision, 1852

The storm that raged along the North East coast at the end of October 1852 meant there was plenty of work for the Seaton Carew, Hartlepool and Redcar lifeboats. As the wind became stronger and the sea higher, the masters of a number of vessels that had weathered the gale out at sea for a day or so decided it would be prudent to make for the shelter of the Tees or Hartlepool. In some cases this was to be a fatal decision. A Rochester brig, *Amulet*, under the command of Captain Grey, foundered about a mile offshore from Seaton Carew with the loss of all her crew. Seven men were seen in the rigging prior to her sinking.

An unidentified galliot also foundered offshore from Seaton Carew with the loss of all hands. A Newcastle brig, *Northam*, was seen to strike the Longscar Rocks so Coxswain William Hood and his crew of sixteen, amongst whom were four of Hood's sons, Will, Robert, Henry and Charles, launched the Seaton Carew lifeboat, *Tees*, and struggled to reach the seamen before the vessel went to pieces. Even though the crew of the lifeboat had the storm, and also the extreme danger from the huge pieces of wreckage being thrown about in the heavy seas, to contend with they managed to rescue seven from the crew of nine from the *Northam*.

Shortly afterwards, a coal-laden brig, *Wensleydale*, struck the rocks in almost exactly the same spot as the *Northam*. Captain Brunswick and the carpenter were hurled into the water and drowned. The lifeboat brought off the bodies of the men who had already died from cold and exhaustion and rescued the mate and a seaman, the only two surviving members of a crew of ten. The young cabin boy had been washed overboard the night before.

The *Queen Victoria* of Sunderland foundered at the entrance of the West Dock. All the crew were saved but for one seaman who had previously been washed overboard at sea.

A North Shields barque, *Brilliant*, was wrecked at Hartlepool. She had already lost the carpenter, Thomas Wilson of Howdon, who had been washed overboard at sea. While the remainder of the crew were coming ashore one of them, an old seaman, had his bag holding his sea boots stolen. Other exhausted seamen were also robbed by unscrupulous locals.

A Rostock brig, *Louise*, under Captain Zeplieu, when trying to navigate into the Tees struck the North Gare. Captain C Day and the crew of the SS *Contractor* managed, at great risk to themselves, to take off seven of the seamen in two attempts. The Redcar lifeboat *Zetland*, which had pulled eight miles to reach the site, then took off the remaining three seamen from the wrecked vessel. Two unidentified vessels were seen to founder off Hartlepool with the loss of all hands.

5. Hartlepool Heugh, 1854

On 3 January 1854 a number of colliers that had been expected at Hartlepool arrived late due to the severe weather. They took their chance at high tide on Tuesday evening to enter the port and all were moored safely. On Wednesday morning the winds had picked up and another fifty or so vessels ran for the port. The scene was of utter confusion with some of the vessels being stranded on the bar and others run ashore on Middleton beach. There were a few collisions due to the density of the ships trying to reach safety. The locals were just breathing a sigh of relief for, although there had been damage to ships, there had been no lives lost. But their relief was premature as, at about noon, with heavy snow falling and winds ESE force 9, the lifeboat was called out to the assistance of a London brig, *Dapper*, which was seen to be heading for the Heugh Rocks. The beach was crowded with spectators as the lifeboat was manned with fourteen men and launched. A groan reverberated through the crowd as the brig struck the rocks before the lifeboat could reach her. The *Dapper* appeared to spring at the rocks and was thrown off again into the breakers. The crew could be seen clinging to the rigging with desperation in their eyes as the brig was pounded against the rocks again and again. The topmasts were gone and the *Dapper* was thrown on her beam ends. The lifeboat tried many times to get near but it was an impossible task as the heavy breakers kept sweeping her further and further away from the spot. One by one, through the haze of snow and sleet, the crew could be seen to fall from their precarious hold. The lifeboat pulled Captain Francis Spencely and the mate, John Bailey, from the water barely alive. The six members of the crew that drowned were George Clarke, Humphrey Watson, George Davis, Phillip Spencely and two youths, James Campbell and 'George' (surname unknown).

During this spate of severe weather around twenty-five vessels were stranded at Hartlepool and Middleton beach, many of which became total wrecks and others sustaining varying degrees of damage.

❦

6. New Year But No Respite, 1856-7

On Friday 26 December 1856 the night was dark but clear and although there was a brisk wind it was by no means gale force. The sea, however, was rough with heavy breakers surging onto the shore. A light was seen from a brig which had struck the rocks at the Hartlepool Heugh. About fifty men were soon at the scene with the rocket apparatus. The first rocket was fired giving the crew a glimmer of hope, only for the hope to be dashed as the lines missed its target. It was decided that larger lines were required and there was some delay before these were brought to the scene. By this time the tide was nearly in full flood and large waves were beginning to wash over the crippled ship. More lines were fired but of those only one landed near to the deck and was not grasped by the crew quickly enough before being swept off again and the others fell far short or the lines broke. In all, five Carte's and six Dennett's lines were aimed at the ship with no success. By this time the tide was nearly in full flood and large waves were washing over the crippled ship. Cries of terror could be heard from the vessel and the distress signal, which had hung from her bow, stopped flashing. As the ship keeled over with terrible creaking and snapping noises the cries of her crew became fainter until only one voice could be heard, then that too eventually fell silent. All that could be seen was the dark outline of the hull being rolled about in the surf.

The following day amongst the scattered wreckage the stern-board was found bearing the name of the vessel. She was the *St Lawrence*, a Canadian-built ship, owned by Henry Mayors of South Shields. Of the crew of ten, seven bodies were washed ashore. Those of the master, John Hodgson, the mate, William Vart, the carpenter, William Stephenson Webster and John Bowman, a young boy, were identified. The inquest on the disaster concluded that the ship should have been able to avoid the rocks so either there had been a fault with the course the master took or the vessel was already damaged, perhaps leaking. It was further concluded that the lifeboat should have been launched and in all probability if this had been done lives would have been saved. However, at the time, the opinion was that the rocket lines could perform the rescue so no blame was laid. It was decided that there was some neglect on the handling of the rockets and that the lines were not in good condition but also that the crew of the *St Lawrence* probably did not have enough strength left to lay hold of the line that did reach the deck.

There was some delay to witnesses' identification of the bodies. It transpired at the inquest that the reason for this was that the owner of the vessel would be responsible for the burial costs of the apprentices. If identification was delayed the parish would bear the cost temporarily which would later be paid by the local council. When this was explained to the coroner he pointed out the grief this delay would cause the families of the deceased. He then made eight witnesses swear on oath and these men were then taken to the dead-house to make the identifications.

The Hartlepool people were still reeling from the events at the end of the old year when the start of the new brought further tragedy and havoc to shipping. This storm brought an unrecorded figure, but it was estimated that 180 lives were lost along the North East coast. On Saturday 3 January 1857 there was just a light breeze blowing but by the following day this had increased to a severe SSE gale. Snow and sleet fell in sheets; the wind raged with unrelenting fury and the waves were described as mountains high. The first incident at Hartlepool was when a Whitby brig, *Stanley*, was driven towards Middleton and came so near to the pier that the crew were able to jump to safety. She was then driven ashore on the sands. A few minutes later the *Chance* of Whitstable was struck by heavy seas and went over onto her side and was drifting near to Carr House at the north end of Seaton. The Seaton Carew lifeboat, *Tees*, under the command of Robert Hood, was launched with the crew of seven being rescued from the hapless vessel. Many ships made it to harbour in safety, sustaining damage varying from slight to severe, and others foundered or were wrecked but with no loss of life. This was to change as the hours marched on. During a particularly heavy hail-storm a light brig was seen to try and make it to harbour. The events could not be seen too clearly because the hail obscured the vision of the observers on shore. One minute it looked as though the brig was going to reach a safe haven and the next her foremast and rigging was gone and she was swept towards the Longscar Rocks. The Seaton Carew lifeboat, *Tees*, was launched but before they could get near, the ship had disappeared under the waves, leaving behind nothing to identify her or the men on board.

Near to the Heugh lighthouse, a schooner was seen battling the waves. She was all but submerged under a huge wave but then seemed to recover until minutes later another wave hit her. All that was left visible was a portion of wreckage floating on top of the waves where she had been. Once again the sea had claimed an unidentified ship and her crew. The *Mary* of Colchester had lost her mast and was drifting towards the Heugh Rocks. The Hartlepool lifeboat was carried a distance of almost three miles by the crew and helpers and then launched to take off a crew of five from the *Mary*. Two other crew members had been washed overboard earlier that day. The schooner *Jubilee* of Guernsey took the ground at the north end of Seaton. The lifeboat reached her and was dashed against the vessel's anchor and severely damaged but still

The Seaton Lowlight which was demolish in 1900. The lighthouse stood just to the north of Staincliffe House at a spot know locally as Lighthouse Corner. The Highlig was at Longhill and from the sea the ligh one lighthouse shone above the other war seafarers of the dangerous Longscar Rock
Hartlepool Arts and Museums

managed to get the crew of six off their vessel and to safety.

The *Empress* of Sunderland was driven onto Longscar Rocks. The Seaton and the West Hartlepool No 1 lifeboats were launched but could not move their boats far from the shore because of the strength of the tide. They battled against the waves throughout the daylight to no avail. Rocket apparatus was made ready but the efforts to use them were fruitless. The ship had broken up and it was thought that all hope was lost for her crew, when, at about 10.30 pm, a large piece of wreckage was seen drifting towards shore and, to it, clung four men, exhausted and benumbed by the cold, but alive. The ship's master and five of her crew had been lost when the ship's two small boats had been swamped earlier that night.

North of Hartlepool Bay, near Easington, the brig *Era* of Rochester was struck by a heavy sea and one of the crew was washed overboard. The vessel was driven on shore between Castle Eden and Horden. She was grounded about forty yards (approx 12m) from land and the crew could be seen to be numb from the cold and exhausted. The mate managed to get out a rope with a cork fender on the end to try and make a link to the shore but it snagged in stones. Some of the men on shore formed a human chain link by holding hands and wading into the huge seas. This was led by a joiner, Henry Houghton, who was later awarded the RNLI Silver Medal for his bravery. By this means the men managed to get hold of the rope and the crew of eight were rescued. The *Era* became a total wreck.

An escape that was thought nothing short of miraculous was that of a Ramsgate schooner, *Johns*. On her reaching harbour it was found that she had been brought through the seething waters to safety by only two of the crew, the rest having been swept overboard in the heavy seas.

When the storm abated the beaches were strewn with stranded and wrecked ships. Amongst them, on Middleton, were the *Native, Nymph, Union* and *Duke*. Seaton Carew was host to the *Hibbert, Empress, Chance, Jubilee and the Ayres*. The loss of life was tragic that day but without the bravery and tireless efforts of the crews of the Seaton Carew, Hartlepool No 1 and No 2 lifeboats it would have been far greater.

7. The Blackhall Rocks, 1860

May 1860 saw the whole of the British Isles affected by a storm in which the winds fluctuated from NW to NE by E, with numerous minor casualties to shipping being reported out to sea along with many vessels wrecked or stranded ashore.

The *Jane Green* was a barque of 417 tons belonging to John Tully and Co of Monkwearmouth. After discharging her cargo of pitch-pine timber at the Royal Dock at Sheerness she had sailed on Thursday 24

This windlass was discovered in 1998 by a man out walking. It is thought possible that it came from the Jane Green which was wrecked in 1860. The rod, which is half a metre in length, shows the size scale. Before the wooden artefact could be retrieved and properly examined it disappeared, either under the sand or washed back out to sea. Tees Archaeology

May in ballast for Sunderland. Her captain was John Henderson Taylor of Sunderland and he had a crew of eleven aboard. Early on the morning of Monday 28 May, Taylor found his vessel in the midst of a violent gale with sleet, snow, rain and a tremendous wind. After battling for some time against the elements the vessel's foretopmast staysail was blown away. Taylor and the mate mistakenly thought that they were south of the Tees and near the Redcar rocks and so tried to drop anchor but one of the chains caught in the windlass and the other got away. The crew tried unsuccessfully to cut the chains. They then realised that their position was not at Redcar but much further north, just near the fearful Blackhall Cliffs, an extremely dangerous place to be during a storm. Having no control over her, the ship was driven onshore near to the Blackhall Rocks, about 200 yards (approx 182m) from the high water mark. The lower hold filled with water and the *Jane Green* keeled over onto her beam ends and began to break up. Taylor and his crew got onto the vessel's broadside and waited for a short time, hoping for assistance as they could see people on the shore. Time, however, was not on their side and some of the crew, including the fourteen year-old apprentice, John Henry Plummer, were washed into the sea. The remaining men knew they had no choice but to try and reach the shore through the boiling surf either by swimming or by taking hold of floating wreckage.

The mate was the first to jump from the ship and the others watched as he swam towards the shore. The captain, who was known to be a strong swimmer, jumped off second. When about halfway to the shore he grasped hold of a piece of timber and had almost reached safety when a huge wave engulfed him and he disappeared from sight. William Blanch and Hugh Pottinger of Hartlepool, Henry Sutton, Paul Calvert and William Kirtley of London were also drowned. Two of these men had each left a widow and four children and one a pregnant widow and three children. The mate, William Watkins from Newport, John Broderick and John Hayley from London, John Poole from Sunderland and Joseph Stafford from Hartlepool, all in a state of utter exhaustion, were dragged from the water by willing hands and escorted to a nearby cottage to be attended to.

Broderick stated at the inquest that he was missing some money, a medal from the Shipwrecked Mariners Society and a comb. These, he believed, had been taken from his pocket while he lay sleeping in the cottage. Stafford said that some of the people ashore seemed more intent on the goods and wreckage they could steal than on assisting the shipwrecked men and that night, while he was sleeping, his belt was cut and his tobacco pouch taken. He added that no rocket lines had been fired towards their ship, no lifeboat was to be seen and there was only one coastguard in attendance upon the shore.

The reason given for no attempt with rocket lines was that the vessel was out of range. The jury at the inquest decided not to pursue the matter of the lack of coastguards as they may have been employed elsewhere and it was a matter that should be dealt with by the supervisor of the coastguard station.

As the *Jane Green* was been driven ashore the surviving crew related seeing a steam-tug approaching and the men on her take to their small boat. The steam-tug, which was the *Robert and Margaret*, was later also driven ashore and nothing more was heard of the four men who had abandoned her.

Within a short distance of the loss of the *Jane Green* a Sunderland brig, *Lalla*, and a Danish galliot, *Catharina*, were also driven on shore about three quarters of a mile north of the southern extremity of the Blackhall Cliffs. The crew of the former were rescued by means of the rocket apparatus and the crew of the latter got themselves off safely. From these survivors there were also complaints of inhospitable treatment by the locals.

<hr />

8. The Great Storm, 1861

The Great Storm began just after midnight on Saturday 9 February 1861. A Sunderland brig, *Rising Sun*, was sailing from her home port to London with a cargo of coal. On board were her captain, Isaac Holden, and a crew of seven. Not far from Seaham she collided with the ship *Express*, which was showing no lights. The mate, William Marns, was entangled in the rigging during the impact and just managed to avoid being crushed by jumping aboard the *Express*. Both vessels were damaged so headed for the safety of Hartlepool Harbour. The *Express* ran aground on Middleton beach and her crew were saved by the lifeboat. The *Rising Sun* was not so lucky; as she tried to take

An engraving from the Illustrated London News *of ships stranded and wrecked at Hartlepool after the Great Storm of 1861. It was said at the time that one could walk on the wreckage from Seaton Carew to Hartlepool without one's feet touching the sand .* Author's collection

shelter in the harbour she struck the rocks under the Heugh just north of Elephant Rock. The lifeboat could not render assistance because of the danger to her on the rocks so a rocket line was fired. It took many attempts before the line reached the ship because of the extreme force of the wind. Eventually, the line hit its mark and was tied to the mainmast but the block fouled and before another line could be fired the vessel's mainmast went. Because it was in daylight and the ship was so close to land those watching the drama from the shore could see everything in detail. The crew shook hands with one another and then a huge wave pounded the ship and the men were gone. But no! Not all! The watching crowd gasped in amazement when, as the wave subsided, they saw a young man kneeling on the deck with a tight grip on the rigging. The crowd thought that he looked as though his hands were clasped in prayer. Another rocket line was fired and the youth, Henry Prosser, was dragged to safety and taken straight to the Friarage to receive medical attention. This was seen as a miracle and became headline news in both the local and national papers with a ballad being written about the event and the youth who survived when all the odds were against him.

A coal-laden London barque, *Cyrus*, in trying to make the harbour struck against the new pier and then drifted to the old pier and broke up. Her crew were rescued by the lifeboat. Also with a cargo of coal, two brigs, *Mirror* and *Princess*, a Shields brig, *Orbit*, and a Hartlepool schooner, *Savannah*, struck on the bar and sank. A schooner and a brig went ashore near the West Dock piers. The lifeboats were able to rescue the crews of all seven vessels. Opposite the new pier, a few yards from the stone buoy, an unidentified schooner was seen to founder taking all her crew down with her.

A London brig, *Express*, struck on the bar and drifted onto Middleton sands against the West Dock pier. During the night, whilst still out at sea, with limited visibility due to the fog, the *Express* had run into another brig which had sunk with all hands. The lifeboat rescued the crews of two brigs that sank in the bay and the crew of the *Elizabeth* and *Sarah*, of Whitby, which went ashore on Middleton sands.

The scene was reported as being one of utter chaos, with the vessels abandoned by their crews and striking one another as they were left to bob around at the mercy of the huge waves. Many of the ships had lost their rudders and much of the rigging and the sails were in tatters leaving the vessels to aid each other's destruction. There were loud cracking sounds as the masts snapped under the fury of the storm and the beaches were littered with wrecks and stranded ships. A later report stated that a person could walk along the beach from Seaton Carew to Hartlepool on the wreckage without his or her feet touching the sand.

Some of the masters and crews would have known that the two Hartlepool harbours could only be entered safely at certain tides. Because of the buffeting their vessels were taking out at sea they could not afford to wait for the tides to change so many of them tried to make for Middleton sands, which was known to be the next safest haven. The danger of this was that if the wind pushed them too far to the south, they would hit the notorious Longscar Rocks. This was to be the fate of many ships during the Great Storm.

The Rising Sun *as she was being wrecked during the Great Storm on 9 February 1861. Elephant Rock can be seen in the centre of the image. This huge feature collapsed on 10 May 1891.* Author's collection

On Saturday 9 February the Longscar and the sea claimed a
Guernsey schooner, *Alliance*, with the loss of all six crew and a North
Shields snow, *Wansbeck*, built at Sunderland in 1840, with the loss of
Captain Richardson, of South Shields, and his crew of seven. About 9
pm a large vessel was seen drifting towards the Longscar but because
of the darkness of the night it could not be ascertained whether she
had gone aground on the rocks. The following morning she was seen
to have foundered, her hull completely submerged. The seaman's
lifeboat went out to her but there appeared to be no sign of life. A little
later the West Hartlepool lifeboat also went out to her but they too saw
no-one alive. Some of the crew of the pilot's boat, however, were
convinced that, because the vessel's rigging was intact, there was a
possibility of survivors. Accordingly, they went to have a look and
found twenty crewmen lashed to the rigging of what was later
identified as the *Kelsey*, of Shields. They had been in that position for
twelve hours and were numb with cold and totally exhausted. All were
transferred to the lifeboat with great difficulty, as some had to be
almost carried, and brought to safety. This was the full crew with the
exception of the young cabin boy who had been washed overboard
during the night. At 4.30 am on Sunday 10 February a Shields brig,
Providence, became stranded at the inner end of Longscar Rocks. The
West Hartlepool lifeboat and the Seaton Carew lifeboat were launched
with Captain Chisholm and his crew of seven being taken off the brig
safely. When the fury of the storm had abated the coxswains were
required to fill in a Return of Wreck with the details of every rescue
attempt and as many details as possible of the stricken vessel. One sad
entry by Robert Hood, coxswain of the Seaton Carew lifeboat, read:

> *Saturday, 9th February, a brig was seen drifting towards the
> Longscar Rocks. The Seaton Carew and the Hartlepool lifeboats were
> launched at the same moment. They used every endeavour to reach
> the crew, but to no avail. In the meantime another schooner also stuck
> on the rocks at the same place. Both ships became total wrecks with
> the loss of all hands.*

The two vessels were lost at the east end of Longscar Rocks and they
and their crew were never identified.

Some of the other vessels that were recorded 'lost' around Seaton
and Hartlepool during the Great Storm were as follows: a Newcastle
brig, *Mayflower*, sailing from Shields and wrecked on the East Gare
sandbank with Captain John Hall and his crew of seven taken off by
the Seaton lifeboat; brigs, *Maria* (with a loss of all four crew) and
Sprite (with the loss of all seven crew); *George Andreas* (with the loss of
all six crew including the master, twenty-seven year-old Allison Crosby
and a seaman, twenty-six-year-old Boyes Cooper); schooners *Venus*
(with the loss of one man of a crew of five) and *Wave* (with the loss of

all four crew); a sloop, *Spy* (with the loss of all four crew); and a full-rigged ship, *Kelso* (with the loss of one man of a crew of nineteen). About forty or more ships were wrecked with about the same amount stranded. Six local lifeboats worked almost non-stop, saving around 600 persons but it is thought that at least sixty sailors lost their lives.

Later that year, on 2 November, a Sunderland barque, *Robert Watson*, became stranded onshore a little to the south of Seaton. The master, William Kare, and five of her crew got off in their own boat with the remaining five men taken off by the Seaton Carew lifeboat, *Charlotte*, before the vessel became a total wreck.

9. The Compass Box, 1865

On Sunday 19 February 1865 snow began to fall heavily and the winds came in from NE which increased in severity as the day wore on. A London screw-steamer, *Orwell*, returning from Shields, made it into Hartlepool with the loss of an anchor and slight damage to her decks from the heavy seas. The *Mulgrave*, sailing from Jarrow had a narrow escape when she was being towed into Hartlepool by the steam-tug *Liberty*. The tow-line broke so the *Mulgrave* dropped anchor and remained in dangerously close proximity to the Longscar Rocks for some time. Heavy seas were sweeping her decks and the crew were in danger of being washed overboard. An hour after high water the steam-tug *Thomas and Mary* brought her safely into port.

The following day a hard wind was blowing from the north and the sea was extremely high, with huge breakers as far as the eye could see. At about 8.30 am a large Staithes fishing smack, *Thomas and Margaret*, was seen coming around the Hartlepool Heugh, no doubt attempting to reach safe harbour. A large crowd had braved the terrible weather when word had spread that the smack was approaching. The vessel lost her steering when the mainsail was caught by the sea and she was driven right across the bay to Longscar Rocks and then to the south where she grounded. The smack was pitching and rolling, sometimes completely covered by the huge waves. The crowd on the shore shouted at the men aboard to stay with their vessel but the advice was ignored and they launched their coble. The small boat was only in the water a matter of minutes when it was swamped and capsized with the loss of all the men. There had been nine men aboard when the smack had left Staithes but only seven were seen to get into the coble. It was assumed that two had already been washed overboard before the vessel had reached Hartlepool. Amongst the drowned were the captain, William Cole, and his son, Thomas.

Among the wreckage washed ashore was the compass box which was pounced on by three men. Others in the crowd grabbed it from them and ran off but were chased and a fight broke out over possession of the prize. The captain's brother was present and claimed that the box should be his but the crowd turned on him. Had it not been for the intervention of a coastguard brandishing a pistol the outcome could have been very nasty. As it was, the coastguard was hissed and sworn at and threatened with stones.

⁕

10. An Accusation of Neglect, 1866

On Saturday 8 December 1866 at about 8.30 am a Newcastle steamer, *Wrecker*, had left port and was at full steam going downriver when she grounded on the South Gare. On board were her captain and a crew of two. From the shore it could be seen that the sea had put out her fires as there were clouds of steam coming from her. Amongst other pilots and observers watching from shore was the coxswain of the Seaton Carew lifeboat, Robert Hood. He used a telescope to monitor the vessel for some time and decided that she was in no danger, especially as there were three steam tugs in the immediate vicinity. Hood had some business to attend to so left to catch a train to West Hartlepool. A little later the vessel appeared to be in trouble so a Middlesbrough tug, *Swan*, tried to get near to take her crew off. The water was too shallow for her to get close so one of the men aboard, George Cowell, against the tug-master's advice, launched a small boat and rowed towards the stricken vessel. Cowell had underestimated the violence of the sea and, before he reached his target, his boat was swamped and he was drowned. The master of the *Wrecker* saw the danger Cowell was in and launched the ship's small boat and tried to reach him, but he was too late. By some miracle the master managed to make it through the swollen sea and was picked up by one of the tugs.

Meanwhile, on shore, John Lister, a Seaton gentleman, later to become keeper of the Buoy-House, knowing Hood was not available to launch the lifeboat, sent a messenger to try and find Reverend Lawson, Honorary Secretary of the Seaton Carew Lifeboat Branch, to tell him that a vessel was in distress and the lifeboat needed to be launched. The messenger returned and told Lister that Lawson was not at the parsonage so he had not been able to make contact. Lister rounded up a crew of five and, manning the small Trinity House boat, managed to persuade the master of one of the tugs to tow them against the tide to within a short distance of the *Wrecker*. They then got close enough to take off the two men that were still aboard and brought them safely to shore. By this time the second coxswain had been notified on the *Wrecker's* plight and had taken steps to assemble his crew but, when he saw that Lister was already near the vessel, the lifeboat launch was abandoned.

Later that day Lister sent a complaint to the Parent Institution of the

RNLI in London. He accused Robert Hood of a culpable act of neglect of duty. His complaint also stated that the master of the *Wrecker* had, in an act of cowardice, rowed off leaving his crew of two to their fate.

An investigation was launched by the Seaton Carew Lifeboat Committee into the circumstances surrounding the events of that morning and the behaviour of the coxswain, Hood. A ship-owner, Mr John Kell, who had great nautical experience and Lord Eldon, Lord of the Manor of Seaton Carew were present at the meeting to listen to the evidence and give their opinion. Hood was called upon to give his version of what took place along with a few pilots, who were named as competent observers that had been watching the vessel from Seaton through telescopes. The subsequent findings were that, before Hood had left Seaton, no-one had felt any cause for alarm as the vessel had shown no signal of distress and did not appear to be in any difficulty. The vessel was aground in shallow water and the tide was ebbing and, even if there had been any problems, there were three steam-tugs near at hand. Hood's character and dedication to duty, up until this time, had been unblemished. His errand in West Hartlepool had not been of any importance, so it was decided that there was no reason for him to purposely go off knowing there was a vessel in distress. Hood was, therefore, exonerated of any blame. It was also decided that the master of the *Wrecker* had not left his vessel in an act of cowardice but rather in an act of bravery. Lister was not pleased with the outcome and accused the Committee of bad judgement but, when the Parent Institution of the RNLI had received all the evidence and conclusions of the Seaton Carew Committee, they agreed that no neglect of duty had taken place and Hood was exonerated of all blame. As for the master of the *Wrecker*, his version of events was believed, so he was also cleared of blame for an act of cowardice.

The drowned man, George Cowell, left a widow, Hannah, and two elderly parents whom he had provided for. The RNLI made a grant of £10 to Mrs Cowell for her husband's act of bravery.

Mr Lister was given an award of thanks inscribed on vellum and his crew of five £2.10s each from the RNLI for their services in saving life.

11. The Tragedy of the *Francais*, 1874

On Tuesday 8 December 1874 a severe NE gale began to blow over most of Britain and by Wednesday a total of nine ships had been wrecked or stranded near Hartlepool. The *Rose* of Whitby drifted onto Seaton beach, the *Branch* of Sunderland drifted onto the rocks where the breakwater was being extended, the *Corsair* of Weymouth, the *Clara Richmond* of Shoreham and the *Isabella Miller* of Ipswich came ashore

Rocket lines being fired towards the Francais *as she was being wrecked at Middleton on Sunday, 13 December 1874.* Author's collection

near the present Newburn Bridge, the *Beeswing* of Whitby grounded on the boulders just south of the pier head at Hartlepool, the *Robert and Mary* of Whitby and the *Providence* of London, had their crews rescued by the lifeboats.

At 3 am Captain Hayling, of the *Hebe* of Littlehampton, put the helm down and ran his ship ashore at West Hartlepool. The Bergen family were fishermen who lived at Middleton. The father and four sons, seeing that the lifeboats were engaged elsewhere and the crew of the *Hebe* were in danger of drowning, formed a rescue party of their own. They fought their way along the open pier that was being lashed from both sides by huge waves. From the pier end, with great difficulty, they eventually managed to throw a rope onto the deck of the *Hebe* by which means they assisted the crew to pull themselves to safety. By this time the ship was filling with water and if it had not been for that brave family the outcome for the crew would have been very different. Miraculously not a single life was lost that day in the waters around Hartlepool, but four days later there was a very different outcome.

On Sunday 13 December a barque, *Francais*, from St Malo in France, was seen offshore, first heading south to Redcar and then north to Blackhall. Her captain, not knowing the area, was checking the best way into harbour. As she sailed around in the bay, although the vessel was being well managed, she was getting closer to the rocks. The tug *Thomas and Mary* approached and offered to tow the *Francais* into harbour for a fee. The captain refused the price the tug-master was asking and offered him much less. The tug approached the vessel a second time but the captain refused his services. During the early evening the *Francais* veered south as if to enter the Tees but baulked at the bar. She then put up a signal to say she needed assistance into harbour. Three tugs approached her with the *Amelia* reaching her first.

A line was made fast and the tug-master intending taking the ship to Old Hartlepool as he considered it safer, turned her in that direction. As this was attempted the line broke and before any more could be done the ship had struck ground at Middleton Sands. Lifeboats attempted for some considerable time to reach the stranded vessel but the cross currents of the tide were too strong for them to render any service.

The rocket apparatus was sent for, but it was well over an hour before it was in place and ready for use. Five rocket lines were fired and, of these, one landed on the deck of the *Francais*. The crew made no attempt to secure it to the mast and it was thought that they had no knowledge of how to utilise the equipment, which was all too often the case. Normally, Middleton was a fairly safe place for a vessel to ground as the crew could wait until low tide and just wade ashore but, as was confirmed by a surveyor later, the timbers of the *Francais* were rotten and within a short time the vessel went to pieces drowning all aboard except one, Francois Aucoin, who was seventeen and the only one of the crew who could swim.

The event caused a sensation and was widely publicised, as far as Denmark, France and Germany, as well as the major towns and cities of Britain. A trouble-making clerk, Carl Peterson, who worked for E A Casper, Consul for the Netherlands, wrote a letter to a Danish newspaper saying that the people of Hartlepool had refused to help those aboard the stricken ship and that the spectators had cheered as she went to pieces. The letter was written as if from eyewitnesses and

In service from 1873-88 and instrumental in saving sixty-seven lives, the Job Hindley *outside the lifeboat house at South End, Seaton Carew with Henry Hood and some of the crew c1875.* Author's collection

was signed by sixteen Danish captains who were in port at that time.

A subsequent inquiry by the Board of Trade into the events found that the cheering had taken place when the *British Queen* and *Coral Queen* had passed to safety through the West Harbour entrance. It was further proved that some of the Danish captains whose signatures were on the letter had not been eye witnesses; in fact one of them had been asleep at the time of the wreck. This shed doubt on the validity of the other signatures or, at the very least, whether the signatories knew what they were putting their marks to. The tug-master of the *Thomas and Mary* should not have tried to barter a price because it was usually a set towage fee. He stated that he had asked for a high price because of the terrible conditions and the considerable danger to himself and his vessel. If there was a subsequent query from any of the masters of vessels on the fees that a tug had charged the matter could be assessed and dealt with by a magistrate or an assessor. It was claimed later by some of the witnesses that it would have been easier for the *Amelia* to have towed the *Francais* into West Hartlepool rather than trying to turn her towards Hartlepool Harbour and that perhaps this had been done so a higher fee could be charged. Other witnesses stated that the tug-master had done the right thing and it had been the safer option. The inquiry gave the tug-master the benefit of the doubt and he was exonerated from blame.

This tragedy prompted changes to the way things were handled regarding the Port of Hartlepool. Recommendations were put forward to improve the law on the way in which tug fees were charged and implemented and the way rescues were co-ordinated by the different bodies concerned. It was also suggested that the RNLI take over the management of all the Hartlepool lifeboats, which was agreed and, shortly afterwards, put in place.

12. Hartlepool Bay, 1880

The final days of October 1880 saw severe weather which affected all of Europe and the British Isles and the waters around Hartlepool Bay were no exception. On 28 October at about 2.30 pm a vessel was observed drifting across the Bay towards the Tees before a fearful sea and ENE gale. She was a Shoreham barque, *Margaret Caithness*, bound from Portsmouth to Sunderland with a crew of nine under Captain John Sharpe. The vessel had both anchors down and, at about 4 pm, she hoisted a signal of distress. The Seaton Carew lifeboat, *Job Hindley*, was taken on the beach opposite the ship about a half mile south of Seaton, where lights were then shown for the captain to slip his cables and come on the beach. The captain and crew did not understand the signal and the barque was driven onto the North Gare where she still kept drifting and striking on the sand. With the position of the ship it was impossible for the lifeboat to get to her. She was anxiously watched all night and at about 5.30 am the captain of the vessel attached a small boat to a buoy with a strong hawser attached. This was hauled aboard the lifeboat and the crew were taken off one by one.

A Sunderland barque, *Zeno*, had been bound from Huelva to Aberdeen with a cargo of sulphur when she was caught in the storm and it was believed she was driven on to the end of the Longscar Rocks. Captain F Moore and his crew of ten were all lost. The bodies of the mate, John Gallagher, and one of the crew were washed ashore near the mouth of the Tees on 30 October.

A Paisley schooner, *Express*, sailing from Runcorn to Newcastle with a cargo of salt, was lost with her captain J Ham and his crew of three somewhere off Hartlepool. The only thing that was known of her was when a board with her name on it washed up at Castle Eden Dene.

The *Cambria* of Sunderland had shown signals of distress and was towed into Hartlepool by a tug, *Scotia*. In trying to battle with the elements all her crew had been injured and her captain, Burton Brown, had been washed overboard. The lifeboat, *John Clay Barlow*, was manned and went out in search of him but returned empty handed.

At about 8 pm a brigantine, *Folkestone*, was seen approaching Hartlepool with her sails gone and burning signals of distress. The Hartlepool No 2 lifeboat, *Charles Ingleby*, was manned and launched. They succeeded in bringing off Captain George Morley and his crew of six before the vessel drifted towards Middleton and was wrecked. A Middlesbrough snow, *John Cock*, was also wrecked at Hartlepool with her crew of seven safely got off.

The French Schooner, Alphonse Maria, *was sailing to Middlesbrough when she struck the Longscar Rocks on Friday 26 August 1881 and was washed onto Seaton beach at high tide. Captain Calmer and her crew of five saved themselves in their own small boat.* Author's collection

Besides damage to ships, loss of life and injuries to seamen, the seas were so violent that the bell buoy was dashed from her position at the end of Longscar Rocks and washed ashore near Carr House at the northern end of Seaton Carew.

13. A Dramatic Rescue, 1883

At about 8.30 pm on Sunday 11 March 1883 a rocket and burning flares were observed from the north side of Longscar Rocks. The signals of distress were from a Swedish brigantine, *Atlas*, which had been sailing from Drammen to Sunderland with a cargo of ice. On board was Captain Cimmermann, who was also the owner, and a crew of four. The wind was strong NE bringing with it heavy showers of snow and whipping the sea into a frenzy. The Seaton Carew lifeboat, *Job Hindley*, was launched and arrived near the distressed vessel shortly before 11 pm. It was not high tide and because of the position of the brigantine on the rocks the lifeboat could not get alongside. It was clear to everyone that if the crew were not taken off quickly they would die as the ship was already beginning to break up. In an amazing feat of courage, the coxswain Henry Hood and John Franklin stepped out of the lifeboat and onto the slippery, partly submerged Longscar carrying a rope that was attached to their boat. These two men were closely followed by Matthew Franklin. At one point Hood was washed from his precarious path and the sea was throwing him against the rocks. John Franklin jumped into the water and managed to tie a rope around Hood and pull him back onto the solid rock. The three men then worked their way towards the *Atlas* until a rope could be thrown onto the deck. The rope was made fast and the lifeboat men and the crew of the brigantine made their perilous way back to the lifeboat using the rope as a stabiliser. When the lifeboat arrived safely back on shore at a little after midnight it was found that Hood was badly bruised from his ordeal in the water. He was also so exhausted that he could not speak. From the safety of the shore the crew of the *Atlas* watched as their ship went to pieces.

Those who had seen the position of the brigantine and knew anything about the dangers of the Longscar Rocks had not believed it would have been possible for the crew to be rescued. All the local papers carried the story of the bravery of the lifeboat crew that had risked their lives for others. The RNLI Silver Medal was awarded to the three men for their bravery and Queen Victoria also conferred the Albert Medal on Hood.

The naming ceremony of the new lifeboat, John Lawson, *performed by the curate, James Pattison on Seaton Green in 1888. The lifeboat was named after the Seaton villagers beloved vicar. This lifeboat was in service from 1888-1906 and was instrumental in saving thirty-four lives.* Pattison's Pictures, Bowes Museum

Reverend John Lawson, vicar of Holy Trinity Church and Honorary Secretary of the Seaton Carew Lifeboat Station, Coxswain, Henry Hood, crew and helpers with the John Lawson *lifeboat in 1888.* Pattison's Pictures, Bowes Museum

14. The Loss of the *Granite*, 1888

At about 9 am on the morning of Tuesday 13 November 1888 the winds were blowing strong SSE and the sea was rough. A brig, *Granite*, with its crew of eight, three of whom were young boys, was on its way to Middlesbrough after sailing from London with a cargo of loam. The *Granite* was owned by Thomas Jefferson of Scarborough Street in West Hartlepool so the crew were looking forward to spending some time in their home port. The coastguard on duty at the Seaton Carew Station saw the vessel drive ashore on the North Gare and immediately fired the distress signal. Within a very short space of time a large crowd had gathered, some to assist and some to observe. The rocket apparatus and the lifeboat on its carriage were taken over the Snook to the mouth of the Tees and the boat was launched with its crew of twelve at 10.15 am. This was to be the first rescue attempt in the new lifeboat, *John Lawson*.

Five tugs had been dispatched from Middlesbrough to aid in the rescue and once the lifeboat got into the channel a tug, *Agamemnon*, took hold of her and towed her to the stricken vessel. Because of the volume of the waves this took almost an hour and by this time the *Granite* was in dire straits. The spectators on the shore could see the sailors clinging for dear life to the rigging and could hear their desperate cries for help. The tug, still keeping hold, dropped the lifeboat to the leeward side of the *Granite*. This was attempted seven or eight times but the current was so strong that the lifeboat kept drifting and the grapnels missing their target. On one throw the spectators on the shore saw the grapnel catch on the rail and then fall. By this time the doomed vessel was breaking up and the crew, one by one, falling from the rigging into the freezing sea. The lifeboat searched amongst

A sketch of the lifeboat, John Lawson, *on her first rescue going to the aid of the* brig Granite *on Monday 12 November 1888. The crew consisted of Coxswain Henry Hood, Robert and William Hood, Robert Robinson, John Kendel, Thomas Blenkinsopp, F Kitson, William Proctor, Matthew Franklin, William Harrison Richard Burton and one other.* Author's collection

the floating wreckage and at one point saw a man with his arm outstretched towards them. They rowed towards him as fast as they could but he disappeared under the waves before he could be reached. The lifeboat and the tugs circled the area for a considerable time but found no one and, having to admit defeat, the lifeboat returned to the shore at about 2 pm with its crew cold, exhausted and heartbroken at the tragic outcome.

The loss of the seamen was all the more heart-rending because they were in sight of home after a long journey. This tragedy did not end with the loss of the crew of the ship; amongst the watching crowd was a Seaton resident, Mary Ann Strover, a lady of seventy years. The events must have been too much for her and she suffered a heart attack and died on the shore in front of her friends and neighbours.

The lifeboat crew on this occasion consisted of coxswain Henry Hood, Robert Hood, William Hood, F Kitson, William Proctor, Matthew Franklin, J Kendel, Robert Robinson, Thomas Blenkinsopp, William Harrison, Richard Burton and Ambrose Storer.

The crew of the *Granite* consisted of Captain Richard Leng, John Richard Steel, H Perkins, W Hartland, D Palmer, D Buckley W Atkinson and seventeen-year-old William Pearson Storm.

The coxswain later reported that the new lifeboat had behaved very well and, in his opinion, his crew and the crew of the tugs had done everything possible to rescue the sailors from the doomed ship.

⚓

15. The *Dauntless* and the *Trio*, 1901

On Tuesday 12 November 1901 once again havoc was wreaked up and down the north-east coast when winds sprang up that blew an ENE force 9 gale. The rain fell in torrents and the wind howled without intermission for three days. The sea was at its mightiest with huge clouds of spray dashing over piers and promenades and battering cliffs relentlessly. The experienced pilots agreed that this was the worst storm they had seen for many years.

At about 4 pm the crew of the Hartlepool lifeboat *Cyclist* were just re-housing their boat after an exercise when a call came in to say a vessel was in trouble near the end of West Hartlepool pier. The Seaton Carew temporary lifeboat *Charles Ingleby* had also just been out on exercise when they received word of the stranded ship. The crew were instructed to stand by in case their assistance was required. The stranded ship was a barque, *Dauntless*, built in 1873 by Spencely at Sittingbourne. She was owned by J Burnham and Smith of Maldon of Essex. Carrying a cargo of railway tracks, the *Dauntless* was sailing with her master, Frank Lucas, and a crew of two, from Kent to Newcastle-

Tombstone in Holy Trinity churchyard dedicated by Rev John Lawson and the villagers to the unknown sailors who lost their lives in the waters around Seaton Carew. The inscription is now almost indecipherable but once read: Around this same stone lie the remains of sailors who perished in the mighty waters and whose bodies were washed on shore from the wrecked vessels. Dedicated by the villagers. Be ye also ready. The Author

upon-Tyne when the storm hit. The ship had lost all but her fore topmast staysail and it was obvious that she was in great danger. The *Cyclist* was launched under the supervision of the coxswain, Thomas Rowntree, but as she was on her way a tug took hold of the *Dauntless*. The lifeboat stood by and after about twenty minutes saw the tug's tow-rope break. The *Dauntless* began to drift so she dropped anchor as the tug tried to get hold of her again. A second tug also tried but both were unsuccessful in securing a rope. The seas suddenly became very heavy and broke over the stricken vessel bringing her anchor home. She immediately began to drift into broken water and cross seas where it was impossible for the lifeboat to follow.

The disabled ship soon began to go to pieces and the three men on board jumped into the freezing sea. All three had lifebelts on and, although ropes were thrown to the men from the end of the pier, it appeared they were too cold and exhausted to keep hold of them or swim and they bobbed about like corks before being drowned and swept away towards Middleton jetty.

The *Trio* was a barque, built in 1868 by G Scotte of Procida, and owned by her captain, Nilsson, who, along with most of his crew of ten, came from Kalmer in Sweden. She had left Hartlepool on the Monday morning with a cargo of coal to sail via Norway back to Sweden. The sea was calm and there was just a light breeze. At about 8 am on Tuesday the light breeze suddenly became a gale. The crew shortened sail and at about 8 pm found themselves eight miles from the Croquet Islands. The *Trio* was steered southward to avoid running ashore and about 11am on Wednesday

Hartlepool Lighthouse, built in 1846 and removed in 1915 during the First World War, because it stood in the way of the guns at the Heugh Battery. It was replaced with a temporary lighthouse until 1927 when the present lighthouse was built. Author's collection

came within sight of Hartlepool. By this time most of the sails were gone, the hatches broken and the ship waterlogged. They waited for high tide and tried to get into Hartlepool but could not make harbour so went back out to sea to try to hail a tug they had seen. In this they were also unsuccessful. They then steered opposite the West Hartlepool lifeboat house, as they did so they lost their rudder so had to cut their rigging to ease the ship. At about 4 pm they struck near the south pier and within a short time the *Trio* went to pieces. The captain and his crew were all thrown into the water. Captain Nilsson tried to swim for shore but the water was freezing and he was exhausted. He managed to get hold of a spar and clung to it for his life. Just as all hope had gone he felt willing hands grab him and pull him to shore.

A few of the younger men who had been watching from the shore had risked their own lives by wading into the sea with ropes to pull the sailors from the water. One was Alfred Gales who lived at Pilot Street in Hartlepool. Gales already held the Royal Humane Society's certificate for the saving of lives. Besides the captain, two other men were pulled out alive and all three were taken to the Queen's Hotel to be cared for. For seven of the crew their journey was to the dead house.

a. *During ENE force 9 gales on Wednesday, 13 November 1901 at about 3.30pm the barque, Trio, is seen at a distance sailing into Hartlepool.*

b. *At about 3.40pm the Trio loses her rudder and became unmanageable offshore from Seaton Carew bridge.*

c. *At about 3.45pm the heavy seas are swamping the Trio from bow to stern and she loses a mast. A crew member jumps overboard and is drowned. It is obvious to all watching that the situation is extremely serious.*

d. *At about 3.50pm the sea has become stronger and rockets are fired but all fall well short of their target. The lifeboat could not be launched because of the high seas. By now the beach from West Hartlepool to Seaton is a black mass of thousands of people watching helplessly as the drama unfolds.*

e. *At about 4pm the Trio loses her second mast.*

f. *A few minutes later the third mast falls as the seas are steadily becoming higher and more furious.*

g. *The Trio suddenly lifts and breaks amidships with the cargo of coal flying into the air. Wreckage and bodies immediately begin to float towards the shore. Locals bravely wade into the boiling seas and, miraculously, three of the crew of ten that had been aboard the stricken vessel are pulled from the water still alive.* Hartlepool Arts and Museums

Lifeboat Saturday began in October 1896 and became an annual event to raise money for the RNLI. The Hartlepool lifeboat and crew were taken to Coventry where the first event took place. Back row, from left to right: Coxswain T Reed, T Hood, M Hastings, J Pounder, JHR Denton, R Corner and bosun J Webster. Front row; Second Coxswain J Sotheran, W Pounder, G Sotheran, J Cambridge, W Horsley and J Horsley. Front row: Walter Mason, Rigger Bowes (RNLI London), Alfred Belk (Honorary Secretary of Hartlepool) and AG Boyle (Organisation Secretary of London). George Colley

One of the dead was the Norwegian steward, Carl Nilson, who had been sailing for fifty years and was to retire when they reached Norway. Little did he realise that his final voyage would end in this way. Four of the dead were married men and the two sailors who were saved were single.

In the days that followed, to the distress of the locals, along with the pieces of wreckage that floated to shore, were boxes of toys, presents and dolls that the crew were taking home to their families for Christmas.

During the three days of the storm's fury two other ships were reported as lost near Hartlepool. The *Cornucopia*, a brigantine, built in 1859 with its owner and master J B Williams and a crew of four, was sailing from Jersey. She was wrecked about three miles north of Hartlepool with the loss of all five men.

The *Catherina*, a ketch, built in 1893 in Germany was sailing from Teignmouth to Leith carrying a cargo of china clay. She was wrecked near the end of the pier at West Hartlepool. The master and part owner B Schulte and his crew of three were taken off by the Hartlepool No 1 Station lifeboat, *Ilminster*, under the supervision of the coxswain, Thomas Rowntree. The ketch became a total wreck.

In December of the same year a further three ships were lost near Hartlepool.

The *Florence*, a brigantine, was built in 1866 by Barker at Sunderland. She was carrying a cargo of burnt ore from London to South Shields when she got into difficulties near the old pier at

A postcard depicting the wreck of the Thomas *at Hartlepool on 30 April 1904.*
Alf Carney

Hartlepool. The vessel eventually drifted ashore onto Middleton and was wrecked. Captain George Williams and his crew of six were taken off by the Hartlepool No 2 Station lifeboat, *Charles Ingleby*, under the supervision of Richard Robinson.

The *Wave Queen*, a barque built in 1870, was carrying a cargo of coal from Shields to Guernsey. She was wrecked near the south pier at Hartlepool with the loss of Captain Lawrence, and his crew of eight. The Hartlepool No 2 Station crew, under the supervision of Richard Robinson, attempted rescue but were unsuccessful.

The *Hannah and Jane*, a schooner, built in 1867 in Wales was sailing from Sunderland to Essex when she was wrecked at Blackhall Rocks. Her captain was Humphries and she had a crew of four. Only one man survived.

❦

The Swedish brigantine Primrose *wrecked on Longscar Rocks between Thursday 28 and Friday 29 November 1907. The captain, OF Johansson, and the crew of five were taken off by the Seaton temporary lifeboat,* Charles Ingleby. *The lifeboat crew consisted of Coxswain John Franklin, William Franklin, James and John Lithgo, George Storer, Roy Grieg, J Elliott, Jerry Hodgson, John Cuthbertson, Albert Anderson, Thomas and James Harrison and Thomas Wake. The cost of the lifeboat services amounted to £35 5s (£35.25p).* Author's collection

16. The Last Voyage of the SS *Clavering*, 1907

Wherever there was loss of life at sea through shipwreck it was tragic. This was particularly so when the SS *Clavering* ran aground as this was to be the largest recorded loss of life from one vessel in Hartlepool waters. Also, because the situation that claimed twenty lives was blamed on human error. At the inquest, that blame was laid squarely on the shoulders of Ernest Harrison, a Tees pilot with five years experience of the river, who had boarded the vessel at Middlesbrough. It was his job to assess the direction and speed of the wind and tidal flow so as to guide the ship safely down the Tees to the open sea.

The SS Clavering *wrecked at Teesmouth. Between Thursday 31 January and Friday 1 February 1907, twenty men lost their lives when she was stranded on the North Gare.* Author's collection

Looking at the events that led up to the last fateful hours of the *Clavering*, one would think there would have been doubts as to the reason given for its demise. The later evidence tended to point to a fault with the steering of the vessel, which may have made her unseaworthy, and perhaps the pilot was used as a scapegoat. This is pure speculation on the author's part and it is left to the readers to reach their own conclusions.

Before leaving Calcutta (where most of her crew had been employed) the vessel had had an accident and underwent minor repair. On entering the Thames on New Year's Day she hit the end of a pier and, once again, repairs had to be carried out. Because these were considered minor incidents no records appear to have been kept as to the cause of these accidents. On Christmas Day of 1906 the *Awu Maru* had gone ashore at Redcar and was not re-floated until 14 January 1907. The *Clavering* was supposed to collect some of the disabled ship's cargo but because of the delay caused in London she was so behind schedule that she could not do so.

At the inquest the Tees pilot stated that when he boarded the vessel at Middlesbrough he was told by the captain that the steering was sluggish. Although this remark and the previous accidents were brought into question, it appears they were given only minor attention at the final inquest.

The *Clavering* was a screw steamer – a schooner rigged and built in 1888 by Messrs Workman, Clark & Company, of Belfast as the *City of Dublin*. She was renamed the SS *Clavering* when ownership of her changed. The steamship was fitted with triple expansion direct acting inverted engines of 350hp combined by Messrs J & J Thompson of Glasgow. The diameter of the cylinders being $25^1/_2$ x 43 x $67^1/_2$ inches respectively (approx 64 x 109 x 170 centimetres) and length of stroke was 48 inches (122 approx centimetres). The ship had a gross tonnage of 3328.36 and registered tonnage of 2154-79 and her dimensions were: length 361.7 feet, breadth 42.7 feet and depth of hold 26.4 feet (110m x 13m x 8m approx). She was owned by the *Clavering* Steamship Company, Billiter House, Billiter Street, London. Messrs Edmund Hazlehurst & Company, of the same address, were designated the managing owners from 28 November 1900. The ship steered by steam, a wheel standard being fitted in a small wheel-house on the bridge which was about five and a half feet in diameter. Her hull and machinery were insured for £26,000 and her cargo – on this trip – for about the same amount.

The *Clavering*, according to official regulations, had been inspected before she left London to sail for Middlesbrough and was found to carry her full compliment of safety equipment. She carried six lifeboats which were properly supplied with oars and fittings, ten liferafts stowed on the after wheel-house, one jollyboat, a full compliment of lifebelts and three compasses, all in good working order.

At 4.50 am on 31 January 1907 the *Clavering* left Middlesbrough Dock bound for Japan and carrying a cargo of about 5,000 tons of pitch and iron and some valuable machinery. Her crew of sixty-two consisted of forty-eight Lascars (low caste workers from India), six Chinese and eight Europeans. The Europeans were Captain James Scott, along with officers William H Pinchin, Herman Bevan and Ralph Sadler, and engineers Donald McPherson, A Mills, J Gaban and Charles Campbell. Also on board was Ernest Harrison, the Tees pilot.

The *Clavering* left Middlesbrough under her own steam and accompanied by two tugs, the *Hero* ahead and the *Challenger* astern. Being a heavy vessel the trio had to proceed very slowly down the Tees. The tugs assisted her to negotiate the bends and, occasionally, she used her own engines to keep her within mid-channel. At about 6.20 pm they reached No 3 buoy. Along with sleet and snow, there was a strong gale from the north and the seas were running NE. Robert

A postcard depicting the SS Clavering *showing the huge seas swamping her decks.* Alf Carney

Douglas Harling, mate of the *Hero*, who was acting pilot because of the tug-master was ill, decided the weather was unfavourable to risk his proceeding any further so the tug was cast off. Soon after the master of the *Challenger*, William Hurdman, also cast off but followed the steam ship to the No 2 buoy in case his services were again required. Believing the vessel to be heading out to sea and on its proper course Hurdman turned the *Challenger* and headed back upriver. Between the No 2 and No 3 buoy Captain Scott slowed the vessel so the pilot, Harrison, could hail the tug to have it take him off the *Clavering* and put him ashore but he was unsuccessful in making contact. The captain then said he was not going to risk landing Harrison in the unfavourable weather so he would have to stay on board until they reached Dover to which the pilot agreed as the captain was not familiar with the waters and Harrison did not think it would be safe to leave the ship until they were past the fairway buoy. John Filburn, the keeper of the South Gare lighthouse, saw the *Clavering* pass at 6.25 am. The vessel was well off course and over to the north-west of the channel. She looked to be in difficulties as she was making no headway and he assumed she had broken down. Captain Scott later stated that her engines were at full speed when the Chief Officer reported to Harrison that they were off course. The pilot ordered to continue at full speed and turn the vessel around to port. The vessel did not appear to have the power to steer against the wind, which was against the right starboard, and did not respond to the port helm. Getting dangerously near the North Gare, Harrison then ordered full speed astern intending to turn the vessel in a full circle to bring her back on course.

The vessel appeared to respond to this manoeuvre but then came the realisation that the ship was not moving and that she was stranded. Within minutes the force of the sea and the wind drove her onto the North Gare sandbank. The sea washed over her, smashing the lifeboats and pouring into the stokehold and the engine room. The Lascar firemen, in their terror, abandoned their posts and rushed from the stokehold to the deck but the engineers kept the engines running at full speed for as long as possible until they finally stopped at about 7 am. By this time it had been high water for about two hours.

Signals of distress were raised from the *Clavering* and the message was relayed from the South Gare Station to the various lifeboat stations. At 8 am the Seaton Carew Station received the message and immediately sent for the lifeboat crew and a team of horses. The temporary lifeboat, *Charles Ingleby*, was drawn by eight of Major Thomlinson's strongest draught horses over the snow covered Snook and launched into the river at about 9.50 am under the direction of the coxswain, John Franklin. Their first attempt to reach the stricken ship failed. The lifeboat was too far south and missed the channel. On the second attempt they managed to reach the *Clavering* and take off fourteen Lascars and the third engineer. It was later suggested that the men should have been taken to the tug that was nearby and then the lifeboat could have returned quickly to the distressed vessel and taken off more of the crew. Franklin stated that would have been foolhardy and would have put the lifeboat crew in great danger. There was the risk of her being driven towards the old wreck of the *Carlo* and, because of the high seas; the lifeboat could have easily capsized if the sea had hit their bow while heading in that direction.

The men from the steamship were landed on shore and taken to the Seaton Hotel where the managers, Mr and Mrs Henderson, made sure they were warm and fed to give them a chance of restoring their strength before being taken to the Seamen's Institute at West Hartlepool. As soon as the rescued men had been landed the lifeboat was re-launched but the crew were exhausted and the seas were becoming stronger. As the boat was nearing the North Gare it was swept into the channel. The tug, *Champion*, picked them up and towed them back to Seaton Snook.

Meanwhile, aboard the *Clavering*, seeing the lifeboat was not returning, the officers and crew attempted to launch their one remaining lifeboat and the jollyboat. As soon as the jollyboat was put over the side she was swamped. The lifeboat was damaged and was carrying water but they managed to get her over the side and the pilot, the second officer and four Lascars climbed in. The small boat was swept up the channel where she was later picked up by the tug, *Rosa Glen*. Two of the Lascars had been swept out of the boat before the tug

A postcard depicting the SS Clavering *after her crew had either drowned or been taken to safety by the lifeboats.* Alf Carney

reached her. The crew of the West Hartlepool lifeboat volunteered to attempt another rescue in the *Charles Ingleby*. She was duly launched and towed by the tug *Hibernia* to within 200 yards of the wreck. They waited almost an hour but could see no sign of life so returned to Seaton Snook.

John William Parker, of the tug *Champion*, had received word of the stranded screw steamer and headed down river reaching the *Clavering* at about 8 am. After towing the Seaton boat to safety he then steamed to the South Gare Station and asked the boatman, George Tribe, to load the rocket apparatus onto the tug so a rescue attempt could be made in that way. This was duly done and the tug managed to come within about 150 feet of the stranded vessel. A rocket line was fired but it was against the wind and passed by the ship. Parker asked Tribe to try again as he had two more rocket lines with him. Tribe refused and asked to be taken back to the South Gare Station. Parker knew his tug could be of no more assistance so began to steam back upriver. As the tug reached No 2 gas buoy they recovered a body from the water. The body was later identified as the Chief Officer of the *Clavering*, William Pinchin, of Clay in Norfolk.

Meanwhile, at Hartlepool Lifeboat Station, although there had not been a request for their assistance, it was decided that given the amount of crew still aboard the *Clavering* they should try to help the Seaton Carew boat in a further rescue. About ninety helpers were employed to haul the Hartlepool No 1 lifeboat, *Ilminster*, from her house on the North Sand over the sea banks and to the Iron Bridge at Throston. A team of horses was then hitched to the boat carriage at about 4pm to pull the boat from the Iron Bridge to Seaton. The convoy set off the five miles by road and when they reached Seaton a fresh team of horses was brought and the boat was pulled the last two miles to the Inner Deep where it could be launched. James Lithgo, second coxswain of the Seaton boat was taken on the Hartlepool lifeboat to act as pilot because he was familiar with the area. The conditions by this time were freezing, with snow, sleet and rain falling intermittently. The helpers, although almost exhausted by now, managed to launch both the Hartlepool and Seaton Carew lifeboats without the aid of the horses. The two boats tried various courses for over an hour to reach the *Clavering* but kept getting caught on the slag bank. They then decided to try and approach from the main channel but the flood tide and cross seas caught them full force. Eventually they managed to get within 100 yards (approx 91m) of the steamer. The heavy seas were washing over the stricken ship, at times almost obliterating her completely. The Hartlepool lifeboat showed a white light to try and attract the attention of anyone left on board. They heard shouting so made further attempts to get near enough for rescue but it was not within their power and they had to abandon the attempt and head for shore. The helpers had been waiting at the Snook and when the lifeboats returned were told to go home and return in the morning after daylight. The crews then walked the two miles or so to the village where the Hartlepool men rested in the Seaton Hotel and the Seaton men went to their homes to wait for ebb tide, or slack water, as it was called.

By the morning the seas had calmed down a little so at 7 am both lifeboats went out to the No 3 buoy and dropped anchor until the tide eased at about 10 am. They then approached the *Clavering* by way of the Inner Deep. The sea was still heavy but the wind had died down and was moderate NNW. The Hartlepool lifeboat took off thirteen men including the master, chief engineer, third engineer, nine Lascars and one Chinese. The Seaton Carew lifeboat took off the eleven remaining survivors.

A postcard depicting the wreck of the SS Clavering *lying at low tide.* Alf Carney

All the survivors were cold, exhausted, drenched and in shock with many of them having to be carried as they were unable to walk on their own. They were taken on the tugs *Glenrosa* and *Champion* to the Middlesbrough Seaman's Institute where they were fed and given warm clothing. From there, four of the crew were taken to the North Riding Infirmary, the officers and engineers were accommodated in the Shepherd's Hotel and the remainder of the crew in Buck's Temperance Hotel in Sussex Street.

Besides the two Lascars that had been swept from the ship's small lifeboat the other fatalities had occurred from the men being washed overboard by the huge waves or from exposure in the freezing temperatures during the night. The below deck crew, because of the high temperature of the boilers and the nature of their work were scantily clad so had no protection against the biting winds and freezing sea that lashed the decks. During the night everything had been swept from the deck except the tiny wheel house. In this cramped space twenty-seven of the crew had huddled together with two of the Lascars succumbing to exposure and dying where they stood. Others had already died on the deck and been washed overboard.

At the formal investigation into the tragedy, held at Middlesbrough County Court in March of 1907, the findings were that the wreck was caused by the wrongful act and default of the pilot Ernest Harrison. Captain Scott was deserving of severe censure for not exercising more vigilant supervision in the navigation of his vessel but it was agreed that he had no knowledge of those waters and relied entirely on the chief pilot. No blame was attached to any of the officers or engineers. Ernest Harrison was ordered to pay £10 towards the cost of the inquiry. The court felt that George Tribe, the boatman from South Gare Station, was also deserving of severe censure for failing to make a second attempt at firing the rocket line and they were at a loss as to his reasons for not doing so. His explanation was that, because of the way the tug was moving about in the heavy seas, any further attempt would have been futile.

Those who lost their lives were Chief Officer William Pinchin, fourth engineer Charles Campbell, Lascars Ab Han, cabin boy Sadi Mumin and Ah Sing, along with fourteen more of their countrymen and one Chinese. More than five weeks later only eight bodies had been recovered, that of Sadi Mumin, aged twenty-four, had washed up at Redcar.

A letter was sent from the owners of the *Clavering* expressing their grateful thanks for the efforts of the lifeboat crews. The RNLI Silver Medal was awarded to Shepherd Sotheran, coxswain of the *Ilminster* and the Second Silver Service Clasp to John Franklin, coxswain of the *Charles Ingleby* for their gallant conduct and repeated efforts to try and save lives.

The cost of the transport and launch of the Hartlepool lifeboat on 31 January came to £93.5.5 (£93.27) with the lifeboat crew being paid 45s (£2.27) each. I could find no record of payment for 1 February. The Seaton Carew lifeboat's costs for both days were £86.8s (£86.40) with the crew being paid 75s (£3.75) each.

The *Clavering* soon disappeared beneath the sea but the event did not end there. Just over a year later, on 9 February 1908, a barque, *Haldis*, was sailing from Norway to Middlesbrough with a cargo of pit-props under the command of Captain Theodore Strersen. She was in tow of the tug *Vixen* in heavy seas when she veered off course and

The Ilminster *and her crew at No 1 Station. In the rescue of the men aboard the* Clavering *in 1907 the crew consisted of Coxswain Shepherd Sotheran, Shepherd Sotheran junior, Frank Sotheran senior and junior, J Webster, EF and George Davison, James Hastings, John and Robert Horsley, Robert Hood, John and James Pounder, Thomas Rowntree, Robert Corner and Robert Cambridge.*
Hartlepool Arts and Museums

struck the wreck of the *Clavering*. She ran aground between the skeleton of the wreck and the broken up boilers. The vessel's bottom was torn out and her cargo washed up river by the tide. Her captain and crew of eight launched their small boat but had no oars and were at the mercy of the sea. Without assistance they faced certain death. The South Gare rocket brigade, headed by Robert Harnwell, took their equipment onto the *Vixen* and attempted to secure a line to the *Haldis*. The second line connected with the wreck and then fell into the water. One of the *Haldis* crew managed to get hold of the line with a boat hook and their small boat was eventually pulled through the water to safety.

The Tees Conservancy Commissioners were responsible for the removal of wrecks that were a danger to other shipping and they sent divers down on numerous occasions to inspect the wreck site of the *Clavering*. It was not until 1925 that an examination showed that the wreck had been dispersed enough to prevent it from being a hazard. One hundred years on only portions of twisted metal remain of the *Clavering* as she lies in her watery grave, beneath a partial covering of her cargo of pitch.

***

17. The Coast Guard and the Villagers, 1912

A three-masted Swedish schooner, *Presto*, which was built in 1867, was sailing from Sodertalje to West Hartlepool carrying pit props. She had left her home port on 17 September 1912 with a crew of eight and neared Hartlepool at about 5.30 pm on Tuesday 1 October. There was a strong wind blowing, preventing the vessel from making port herself. A tug went to her assistance but twice the tow-rope broke. A second tug threw the vessel a rope but this also broke. Another attempt was made and on this occasion the rope was made fast. The *Presto* hoisted her sails and the tug began to make for Middlesbrough, which seemed to be the best option, but within a short time this fourth rope also broke. The captain had no choice but to instruct the crew to drop the two anchors. When this was accomplished it was found that the vessel was touching bottom and was going down by her stern onto the Slag Wall at the north side of the Tees.

The Seaton Carew lifeboat crew under the coxswain, John Lithgo, were immediately called but, because of the position of the vessel, they could offer no assistance by means of a boat. The Seaton Carew Rocket Brigade was called out at about 7.15 pm and they proceeded to the Snook with their apparatus under the direction of a Hartlepool coastguard, Harry Cross. There were a number of local people already on the scene. By this time the vessel was being tossed about by the high

A postcard depicting two Seaton Carew officials, the seven surviving crew and the cargo of pit props after the wreck of the Swedish schooner, Presto, *on Friday 1 October 1912 after striking the rocks at the Slag Wall.* Author's collection

waves and the mast was swaying backwards and forwards. The ship keeled over and the mast ended up leaning over the Slag Wall. Two of the crew gripped the mast and were making their way along it hand after hand when it broke. One man was pulled off onto the Slag Wall but the other fell into the freezing waters. A line was immediately thrown to him and he was pulled to safety. The rescuers then managed to throw a line onto the vessel and one of the crew fastened it to the broken mast. With the connection secured, one by one the men were pulled off with the villagers, many of them young women, pulling the rope tight in a tug-of-war fashion to try and keep the mast steady until all the crew were safe.

A postcard depicting the masted, fully rigged, iron ship Otra *stranded opposite the Hartlepool sea wall on Wednesday 12 June 1912. Eight of the crew left in the vessel's small boat with Captain Endre Hefness and the six remaining crew being taken off by the Hartlepool lifeboat* Charles Ingleby. Alf Carney

A postcard depicting the Otra *as she was floundering.* Alf Carney

By about 9 pm the seven exhausted crew had been taken by cab and comfortably lodged at the Seaton Hotel under the care of the landlord, S Swain, and his wife. One of the crew, a young apprentice, was very weak and had suffered a severe injury to his arm. Except for the mate, the crew were confined to bed for a few days, through exhaustion and also because their clothing had been ripped to shreds. Wearing apparel was found for them and all eventually recovered.

The mate, on being brought to safety, told his rescuers that the captain, Johan August Svenson, had gone overboard before the rescue had taken place. Henry Graham Barnet, of Victoria Street in Seaton, walked along the shore line to see if there was any sign of the captain. Eventually he saw a man floating face down in shallow water amongst piles of wreckage. Barnet waded out and pulled the man to shore then blew a whistle for assistance. Artificial respiration was applied to the still warm body but to no avail. It was thought, by the bruises and injuries the captain had sustained, that he had been knocked unconscious by the floating wreckage which had caused him to drown.

A newspaper report at the time, and then repeated years later in 1968, gave the captain's cause of death as being the last man off the vessel, whilst crawling along the mast had fallen to the rocks below. At the inquest held at the Seaton Hotel on 3 October 1912 the mate, Carl Cedergren, disputed this version of events. He stated that as they touched the Slag Wall all hands were on deck and the captain had a light in his hand. The mate then saw him at the doorway to the cabin which was filling up with water. He lost sight of the captain for a few

The cargo of pit-props that littered the beach had been jettisoned from the Otra *by the captain in an effort to re-float the ship.* George Colley

The salvage crew at work on the Otra. George Colley

The Time, *a new hulk, was being towed to Richard and Westgarth's at Hartlepool to have engines fitted when the tug's tow-rope broke and the ship was stranded on Seaton Carew beach on 12 July 1912. She was re-floated and continued her journey to the engine works and was still in use until at least the end of the Second World War.* Author's collection

minutes and then, seeing him in the sea, tried throwing a line but the wind kept it from reaching its goal and the captain disappeared from his sight.

The vessel went to pieces only seconds after the last man was got off and pit-props and wreckage strewed the shores for days until it could all be salvaged. Amongst the debris, one of the articles recovered, was the ship's clock which had stopped at 7.45, exactly the same time as the watch found on Captain Svenson's wrist.

18. The Last Masted Sailing Ship, 1930

On the morning of Friday 26 September 1930 local Hartlepool people woke to a strong NNE gale which had whipped the sea into a frenzy of huge waves that battered against the rocks and the piers. The outlook was dull and grey with the rain lashing down and an icy chill in the wind.

At about noon the local coastguard telephoned the house of Robert Hood, the coxswain of the Hartlepool No 3 Lifeboat, *Elizabeth Newton*. Hood and the second coxswain Frank Sotheran were working at the boathouse and the motor mechanic, Frank Sotheran junior, along with a few other members of the crew, had just left the premises to go for their dinner. As the message was being relayed to Hood the coastguard fired the signal guns, which was heard by the absent members of the crew, who returned to the boathouse immediately. The

The Swedish schooner Doris *which was wrecked at Teesmouth on Friday 26 September 1930. This was the last masted sailing ship to be wrecked in this area.*
George Colley

telephone call had stated that a vessel had been seen in Hartlepool Bay drifting south and dangerously near to the Longscar Rocks. The ship was the *Doris*, a 218 ton three-masted schooner from Thuro in Sweden, which had been sailing with a crew of nine from Wick to load up with a cargo at Hartlepool.

The crew of the Doris *who were rescued by the Hartlepool No 3 lifeboat,* Elizabeth Newton. George Colley

The *Elizabeth Newton* was launched at about 12.35pm and proceeded through tremendous seas towards the vessel. With great difficulty the lifeboat was manoeuvred alongside and Hood spoke through a megaphone to Captain Soren Kobke asking him if he would leave his ship but the Captain replied that he did not want to leave. The lifeboat was then driven southward and the crew fought to return alongside the *Doris*. Hood again spoke to Kobke explaining to him that his ship was very near the Longscar and if she struck the rocks the lifeboat would not be able to get near to assist. After asking some questions on his ship's exact locality in conjunction with the entrance to the Port of Hartlepool, eventually, the Captain grasped the seriousness of his situation and agreed that he and his crew should accept assistance from the lifeboat. Once again the lifeboat was washed away from the ship and had to approach a third time. The crew of the *Doris* now had lines ready to throw to the lifeboat but, again, she was pushed southward and out of reach. On the fourth attempt to reach the ship one of the lifeboat crew managed to throw a small line, which reached its target, and to this, the men on the *Doris* attached a large rope. The lifeboat crew hauled the large rope back to their boat and by

The Elizabeth Newton *and her crew at the boathouse at No 3 Station. The coxswain of the lifeboat,* Robert Hood, *was awarded the Bronze Medal in appreciation of his courage and skill in rescue of the crew of the* Doris. Hartlepool Arts and Museums

The Elizabeth Newton *and her crew out on exercise.* Author's collection

this means were able to draw alongside the ship.

There was no time to waste so immediately, one after the other, eight of crew of the *Doris* jumped into the lifeboat. As the ninth man was about to jump a huge wave washed him back onto the deck. The lifeboat crew held on to the rope and pulled as close as they could to the side of the ship. The last man managed, this time successfully, to jump, landing in the arms of the second coxswain.

After battling with the heavy seas the *Elizabeth Newton* reached the safety of the shore at about 1.35 pm to the clapping and cheering of the huge crowd which had been watching and waiting throughout the drama. The grateful crew of the *Doris* were looked after by the agents of the Missions to Seamen and the Shipwrecked Mariners Society.

The deserted schooner drifted south, and, although it missed the Longscar Rocks, it was driven ashore near the North Gare and became a total wreck. At low tide, depending on the volume of sand, parts of the wreck can still be seen from the shore. This was to be the last masted sailing ship to be wrecked in the vicinity of these waters.

The crew that manned the *Elizabeth Newton* consisted of coxswain Robert Hood, second coxswain Frank Sotheran, acting bowman Ben Rowntree, assistant motor mechanic Frank Sotheran junior, Jacob Hood and Thomas Gilchrist.

19. Gallantry Medals

1826: Silver Medal to George Grey in connection with a shore boat case when five people were rescued from the brig, *Economy*, on 11 October 1824.

30 October 1851: Silver Medal to William Hood, coxswain, for attending thirty-two wrecks and assisting in saving the lives of 120 persons.

1857: Silver Medal to West Hartlepool joiner, Henry Houghton, in acknowledgement for him risking his life by wading into the surf and rescuing seven of the eight crew of the Rochester brig *Era* which was wrecked off Hartlepool on 4 January 1857.

1863: Silver Medal to Robert Hood for saving seven from the Whitby brig *Regalia* when she was wrecked on the North Gare on 12 April 1883 and for long and gallant service in forty-three launches as coxswain.

1869: Silver Medal to Thomas Dawson and a monetary award to the crews of his three steam tugs for safely assisting to harbour fifty-one fishing boats which were in danger of being wrecked on 16 June 1869.

2 May 1883: Silver Medal to coxswain Henry Hood and boatmen John and Matthew Franklin for their extreme bravery in saving the crew of five from the brig *Atlas* on 11 March 1883. Queen Victoria also conferred the Albert Medal on Henry Hood and all the crew received monetary tokens from the Consul General of Sweden and Norway and from two private donors for the same rescue.

1890: Silver Medal to Thomas Pounder, pilot, and James Metcalfe, his assistant for the rescue of two persons from a boat which had capsized near Longscar Rocks on 26 May 1890.

1898: Second Silver Service Clasp to coxswain Henry Hood on his retirement in recognition of his long and valuable service.

1902: A monetary award was made by the German Emperor to the crew of the *Cyclist* for services to the German galliot *Catherine* on 14 November 1901.

1903: Silver Medal to John William Rowntree for the rescue of four from the Montrose ketch *Young John* on 6 July 1903.

1907: Silver Medal to Shepherd Sotheran for the rescue of thirteen from the SS *Clavering* on 1 February 1907.

1907: Second Silver Clasp to John Franklin for the rescue of twenty-six from the SS *Clavering* on 30 January and 1 February 1907.

This photo was taken in 1888 and depicts the wreck of a wooden sailing ship on Seaton Carew beach. Usually every part of the vessel would be salvaged and sold at auction to recover part of the costs of the loss. In this image a large piece of valuable timber remains. It has been suggested that it was left so that when the tide covered the hulk this piece could be seen and would act as a marker so fishing cobles would not strike the wreckage. Pattison's Pictures, Bowes Museum

In August of 1996 the remains of this sailing ship was discovered on Seaton Carew beach. A change in weather patterns due to a recent storm had uncovered the wreck that had lain undisturbed for many years. As sand was rapidly reclaiming the site Tees Archaeology called in volunteers from the Rapid Response Register , a joint project set up by Tees Archaeology in conjunction with the Northern Region Nautical Archaeology Society, to assist them in recording as many details of the wreck as possible. The wreck appears to be a collier brig and is facing landward so was either driven ashore by bad weather or beached by the captain to save the lives of his crew. This is the most intact wooden shipwreck to be discovered on the North East coast and the site has been designated a Historic Wreck Site. By comparing the locations it is possible that this is the same wreck as in the previous image. The Author

1930: Bronze Medal to coxswain Robert Hood for the skill and courage shown in the rescue of nine from the Danish schooner *Doris* on 26 September 1930.

1942: Gold Medal to coxswain Lieutenant WH Bennison, Silver Medal to motor mechanic HW Jefferson and Bronze Medals to each of the other six members of the crew for the rescue of five persons from the steamship *Hawkswood* on 26 January 1942.

1972: Bronze Medal to ILB crew member D Gibbon and the thanks of the Institution inscribed on vellum to helmsman Michael O'Conner and crew member Ian Holdsworth for the rescue of a sixteen-year-old youth when his sailing dinghy capsized on 1 October 1972.

1985: Bronze Medal to coxswain Robert Maiden for his courage, determination and seamanship when the lifeboat landed four crew from the Dutch cargo ship *Anne* when she went aground on Longscar Rocks on 10 November 1985.

Part II

Seaham
and Sunderland

The coastal town of Seaham Harbour was built in 1828 by Charles Stewart, third Marquis of Londonderry, so that his coal could be shipped from his pits at Rainton. The four miles from Rainton to Seaham Harbour were connected by railway. When new collieries were opened in Seaham and Seaton houses were built for the workers. The Marquis died in 1852 but his widow carried on with the construction her husband had begun.

The local pilots were known to often go out in their own cobles to render assistance to vessels in distress. In 1855 the Marchioness of Londonderry agreed to fund a lifeboat for Seaham Harbour. This was provided with some assistance from the RNLI who also supplied the lifebelts and agreed to supply a second set of lifebelts if the Seamen's United Friendly Association could raise the funds for another boat. There appear to be no surviving records as to the size or name of the first Seaham lifeboat but the one provided from funds raised by the seamen was built by Mr Hawkesworth of Torquay and was named *Friend of all Nations*.

In February 1870 the RNLI were approached by some of the local residents and asked to establish a lifeboat station at Seaham Harbour. The Marquis of Londonderry had died in 1865 and the estates were passed to the Marquis Earl Vane who donated the boathouse and the site on which it was built. In April 1870 new RNLI lifeboat *Sisters Carter* of Harrogate was put on display to the public at Harrogate before being sent to Seaham Harbour in September 1870. She performed many rescues before being sold locally in 1887 and replaced with a self-righting boat built by Watkins and Co of London and funded out of a legacy from W H Skynner of London. The lifeboat was named the *Skynner*, after the benefactor, and gave service until 1911.

In 1908 building began on a new deep water slipway and boathouse at the new South Dock. The *Bradford*, a motor lifeboat which had been stationed at Seaton Snook for two years, was overhauled and moved to this station. In 1911 the *Bradford* was once again overhauled and then sent to the Teesmouth Station. In the same year the Skynner was

An extract of a map from the Wreck Register of 1884-5 showing the wreck sites marked with a cross. Author's collection

withdrawn from service and replaced with the *Elliot Galer*, provided from a legacy of the late Mr E Galer of Walton-on-Thames. This boat gave service until 1936.

In 1979, because of the new, high-powered lifeboats that were being built, it was decided that Hartlepool to the south and Tynemouth to the north would be able to deal with any emergencies that arose within the vicinity. Seaham RNLI Lifeboat Station was closed in February of that year after the crews having gone out on service 137 times and saving 289 lives.

Sunderland Lifeboat Station was established in 1800 with the RNLI taking over the station in 1865 when they supplied a lifeboat at the request of the local seamen. Since then there have been seven different stations, mainly due to the fact that it was difficult to find a suitable site. From 1873-87 there were four stations in use at the same time. In 1912 a motor lifeboat station was introduced which is the only station that remains to the present day.

Sadly, few surviving records have been found giving the names of the lifeboats, their donors or the number of lives that were saved from any of the Sunderland stations in the early years. The existing records show that on the south side there was a fishermen's lifeboat in service from 1845-50. The Roker No 1 Station was in use from 1800-1900 with four boats preceding the *Good Templar* which was in service from 1873 and replaced by a boat of the same name in 1876. The *William Hedley*, from 1889 to 1900, was the last boat to be in use at this station. South Side No 1 Station was in use from 1808-43 with one boat in service. South Side No 2 Station was in use from 1819-51 with one boat in service. This became No 1 Station from 1850 until its closure the following year. South Side No 2 Station was in use from 1850-1864 with the service of one boat. The Seamen's Association had one boat from 1856-64. No 3 Station was sited at the south pier from 1858 to 1900 with the first boat being the *Duke of Wellington* which was in service until 1865. This was then replaced with the *Florence Nightingale*. The last boat on this station was the *Junius* which was in service from 1892 until 1900.

On the north side No 2 Station was in use from 1866-87 with a total of three boats in service. No 4 Station sited at the south outlet was in use from 1872-1912. From 1872 the *John Foulston* was in service and replaced by the *Caroline Clagett* in 1887. The *Richard and Nellie Hodges* followed in 1894 with the last boat, *Nancy Newbon*, taking over in 1908. North Dock Station was in use from 1900-16 with the service of the *John and Amy*.

20. Fire on Deck, 1794

During both January and February 1794 NNE hurricane force winds sprang up accompanied by thick showers of snow. The *Ann* was lost offshore from Sunderland, the *Dove* of Christchurch was also lost taking all her crew with her. A London brig, *Kingston*, under the command of Captain Mitchell, was driven ashore and wrecked at Seaham. The *Nautilus, Alexander, Tyro* and *Dorothy* were stranded between Seaton Point and Sunderland.

The loss of a vessel did not always occur because of bad weather. Often there would be other factors such as un-seaworthiness, collision or fire. During the storms February storms a brig, *Good Intent*, under the command of Captain Armstrong was moored at the top of Sunderland harbour when she was seen to be on fire. There would probably have been severe losses had it not been that it was high tide at the time. Several other vessels that were moored beside her were able to be moved to a safe distance away from the burning hulk. The *Good Intent* was then towed into the middle of the river where she could cause no further damage. The fire caused four of the guns aboard, which had been loaded with powder, to go off, sending the watching crowd scuttling for cover. Although great exertions were made the flames could not be extinguished and the vessel, after burning for some time, was sunk.

It later transpired that the fire had been started by a young boy playing on the deck of the vessel. When he left he had not extinguished the lamp he was using and the flame had set fire to the wood.

An engraving of Seaham Harbour in the nineteenth century. Author's collection

21. The Monkwearmouth Pilots, 1852

The storms at the end of October 1852 saw many stranded and wrecked ships at Sunderland. The waves were becoming so high that the keeper of the south lighthouse, Thomas Bolton, was compelled to abandon his post. A short time later a brig, *Beaver*, which had sailed from Hamburg, struck the south pier and, badly damaged, was driven up the harbour to fill with water and sink. All of her crew got off safely. Following this a galliot, *Rebecca Johanna*, also from Hamburg, struck in almost the same spot and was driven behind the pier. Captain Russ and his crew of eight were rescued with the use of Carte's rockets. A Sunderland brig, *Napoleon*, struck the south pier end and was then driven with immense force against the north pier. She began filling with water and, within a few minutes, sank. One man was pulled to safety as he was washed near to the pier. Another man was seen clinging to some spars and shouting for help but none was forthcoming and he was soon washed out to sea. The captain, Palmer, and one of the crew were also clinging to the floating spars. They were seen by William Welsh, Alexander Campbell and William Ward, all pilots from Monkwearmouth. These three bravely took their coble through the heavy surf to rescue the two men. Welsh got hold of Palmer and he was pulled into the coble. They then drew alongside the other man but he was near to death and could not sustain his hold on either the spar or the arms that reached out to him. He slipped from the spar and sank out of sight. Captain Palmer was taken to the *Globe Tavern* on the North Shore where he was looked after by the host and hostess.

The previous day a French lugger, *Melancholie*, had left Sunderland harbour to sail for Boulogne. The captain, Jean Urbin, had been advised by the Sunderland pilots against setting sail because of the forecast of an impending storm but he had ignored the warnings. When at sea the storm had forced him to turn back and endeavour to make for the shelter of the harbour. The lugger struck the south pier and was then driven against the north pier. The heart-rending cries for help of the crew could be heard mingling with the noise of the storm and the creaking and snapping of the severely damaged vessel. Within minutes the ship keeled over under a huge wave and six of the crew disappeared. One man managed to climb up the rigging and cling on. A rocket line was fired but the man was too cold and exhausted to take hold of it. A few seconds later the masts gave way and the man was plunged into the sea. Another man was seen clinging to a spar behind the south pier. A rocket line was fired over him but, he too, must have been powerless to take hold of it and he was washed away in the rolling surf.

This lugger was said to have been ill-fated as, on a previous occasion, during a storm, three members of one family were drowned in the cabin. Friends of that family had petitioned to have the name of the vessel changed to *Melancholie*. The change of name had not brought better luck to the vessel as amongst those drowned on this occasion were a father and his two sons.

The mate of a brig, *Zillah*, was washed overboard by a huge wave as the vessel entered the harbour and a member of the crew of a brig, *Sarah Ann*, met the same fate. In all fifteen seamen lost their lives within view of Sunderland harbour during that storm.

A North Shields brig, *Friendship*, a South Shields brig, *John and Amelia*, an Ipswich sloop, *Thomas Clarkson*, and a Sunderland brig, *Messenger*, all came to grief but with no loss of life.

The absence of the lifeboat caused public condemnation especially relating to the loss of the crew from the *Napoleon*. It was strongly believed that if the lifeboat had been launched more than two men may have been saved from the crew of seven. The reason given for the lifeboat's absence was that there was insufficient crew to man it. During the worst of the storm there were only four men on the pier and they did their utmost to perform rescues with rockets and life lines. They were Thomas Bolton (south light keeper); Snaith (rocker keeper); W Davison (coxswain of the lifeboat) and a mechanic.

During the same storm a Colchester schooner, *Fancy Lass*, was wrecked at Souter Point near Whitburn with the loss of Captain Cole and his crew of five.

22. A Catalogue of Catastrophes, 1854

By the late afternoon of Tuesday 3 January 1854, with temperatures below freezing, a strong wind from ESE had begun to blow. That evening five vessels, with difficulty, made it to the safety of the harbour. On the following tide the *Albatross* of Sunderland was driven on the bar and her crew had to be taken off with the aid of rocket lines thrown from the end of the south pier. The following morning, although damaged, pilots were able to board the vessel and bring her into harbour. Just before dawn on Wednesday morning another fifteen or so vessels made it into the harbour but as daylight broke so did disaster. There were almost 100 ships offshore from Sunderland waiting to enter the harbour to avoid the severe weather so, as soon as the signal was displayed from the lighthouse, vessel after vessel pressed towards the port. Many of them anchored abreast of the dock entrance so that it would be easier and quicker for them to continue their voyages when the weather moderated. However, as the number increased at the entrance, this caused the channel to become blocked and was the

The lifeboat Sisters Carter of Harrogate *on display to the public at Harrogate in April 1870 before being sent to Seaham Lifeboat Station.* Author's collection

beginning of a series of catastrophes to the vessels still trying to reach safe harbour. Some were in collision with each other and sunk while others were stranded ashore on the Potato Garth. These included the *Content* of London, the *Kate* of Leamington and the *Mary Clark*. The first to fall victim outside the harbour was the *Maria* of Montrose which came into contact with the end of the north pier and was thrown high against the breech. The *Harvest* of Sunderland with her bowsprit gone and her bulwarks badly damaged was thrown violently against the *Maria*. The *Zillah, Pilot, Helen Cook, Good Intent, Mary and Jane* and *Jane*, all of Sunderland, the *Mary* and the *Friends* of Whitby, the *Medina* of Cowes, the *Mary Ann* of Seaham and the *San Francisco* of Italy all struck the end pier and followed the first two ships into the

Seaham Harbour in the early twentieth century. Author's collection

same corner. The *John Murray*, *Devonshire* and *Catherine Green* also went ashore behind the south pier.

The thirteen crew of the Italian brig, *San Francisco*, were so frightened by their ordeal and in such a desperate hurry to get off the vessel that they left behind all their belongings. The British pilot that had been aboard since the ship had left the Thames sent a group of men to retrieve the crew's possessions and whatever else could be saved before the vessel became a total wreck. Sadly, with only a few exceptions, this group of men were dubbed the Cornish Wreckers as most of them stole whatever they could lay their hands on. Money, tobacco and Italian ornaments were some of the articles that were taken. Three of the thieves were later caught and prosecuted. The wreck of the hull of this vessel was sold for £125 although the estimated value was £2,000.

The cost in shipping during the storm was considerable, with some of the vessels being totally wrecked and others very badly damaged, but thankfully there were no lives lost at Sunderland.

❦

23. The Sunderland Piers, 1856-7

An iron screw-steamer, *James Hartley*, which belonged to the West Hartlepool Steam Navigation Company, had been sailing from Cronstadt to West Hartlepool in November of 1856. It was late at night and pitch black when, about three miles abreast of Sunderland, the lookout spotted a vessel, under canvas, coming towards them on a collision course. Captain Baldwin immediately ordered the engines to be reversed but it was too late and the two vessels collided. The *James Hartley* had suffered some damage including the loss of her bowsprit

A postcard depicting the Seaham lifeboat, Elliot Galer, *which gave service from 1911 until 1936 and was instrumental in the rescue of fifty-nine lives.* George Nairn

A postcard depicting the Seaham lifeboat, Elliot Galer, *with her crew.* George Nairn

and jibboom, but was still seaworthy. Of the other vessel there was no trace but, miraculously two of her crew managed to make it to the deck of the steamer and were taken safely into port. From these two survivors, one of whom who was the mate, it was ascertained that the sunken vessel was a Shields brig, *Messenger*, which had sailed from London and had been heading to her home port. She had been wind-bound for some time, along with many other vessels, in Burlington Bay and had only left there the previous day to sail for home. Captain Peter Park, four of the crew and the cabin boy had all drowned.

January 1857 heralded a storm which brought huge waves crashing over the pier at Sunderland. A brig, *Rienzi*, had left her Sunderland port but when just a little way out to sea got into difficulty. Her ballast shifted and, becoming unmanageable, she was driven over the rocks at Henden Mill. A rope was brought and lowered over the cliffs to the deck of the ship. One by one the crew were brought up by means of the rope fastened around their waist. One man hit a projectile of rock as he was being hauled up and sustained a nasty wound to his side but otherwise the rescue was a success. A schooner, *One*, of Sunderland, was driven onshore near Ryhope Dene and a brig *Emily*, also of Sunderland, was driven onshore at Hawthorn Dene with both crews being saved.

On Sunday evening the Commissioners of the River Wear had rocket apparatus ready on the north and south piers in case of any incidents where assistance was needed. Three vessels had entered the harbour safely, but one, *Jeanette and Mary* of Shoreham, struck against the south pier. The tiller was thrown from the captain's hand and hit a young man, George Raffle. He was found to have suffered a fractured skull and he died later. The vessel managed to make harbour but was damaged and she filled with water and sank at North Sand.

A French schooner, *Trois Seaurs*, commanded by Captain Le Sauvey, was driven onshore behind the south pier. The sea was dashing over her and the crew were in very real danger. John Sides, one of the Commissioners' men fired a rocket line. It missed its target so another was fired immediately but the crew, although they fastened the line to the rigging, did not know how to handle the equipment. Joseph Hodgson, a carver, volunteered to go to the ship through the surf. This brave man managed to reach the vessel, get on board and arrange the equipment so all the crew were taken off safely by cradle.

The *Apollo* of Southampton struck the pier and was badly damaged. On impact the helmsman was struck on the head with the tiller and died from his injuries soon afterwards. The vessel sank before she could be berthed. A barque, *Harmony*, of Liverpool, drove onto the Ross Sand with the loss of one man. A brig, *Don Quixote*, was wrecked near Seaham Harbour. All of her crew of nine were safe. A Perth schooner, *Blossom*, also foundered offshore from Sunderland.

⟡

24. Disaster for a Fleet, 1861

On the afternoon of Friday 8 February 1861 a fleet of ships left Sunderland harbour in moderate weather. The direction of the wind suddenly changed from NE to ENE bringing with it heavy rain. Throughout the night the wind blew with increased violence and the

A sketch of a brig moored at Sunderland Harbour in the nineteenth century.
Author's collection

rain turned to sleet and hail. At about 4.30 am the *Conrad*, a coal laden brigantine, came ashore about 200 yards south of the south pier. The master Robinson and his crew of three were safely taken off using the rocket apparatus but the vessel was driven well up the beach and became a total wreck. Her cargo was strewn about and was quickly collected by the locals to use on their fires. At about the same time the *Rose* of Hartlepool missed the south entrance of the dock and was driven on shore near the Blue House at Hendon with her crew being rescued without too much difficulty. Many ships came safely into the harbour but almost all had suffered damage of one sort or another. On Saturday afternoon the *Snowdrop* of Portsmouth arrived with the cabin boy and master from the ill-fated Dundee schooner *Wave*. About 8 o'clock that morning Captain Hudson and the crew of the *Snowdrop* had spotted a ship about eight miles from Tynemouth waving a signal of distress. Her mainmast was gone and she was leaking badly. Her pumps were choked because her ballast had shifted and they had been obliged to cut the mainmast away. A line was thrown from the *Snowdrop* and was caught by the crew of the *Wave*. An old man tied the line around his waist and was pulled towards the *Snowdrop* but when the man was dragged on board it was found that he was dead. He had tied the line with a claw hitch instead of a bowline knot and the line had tightened around him cutting off his supply of air causing him to suffocate. The crew of the *Wave* then launched their small boat but as the mate climbed in the boat was swamped and overturned. The mate tried to keep swimming until he could be assisted but his heavy boots and coat would have weighed him down and he was soon drowned. The two ships were now very close together and a boy and a man got onto the jibboom. The vessel lurched as a large wave hit and the boy fell onto the deck of the *Snowdrop* but the man fell into the sea and disappeared. There was only the master remaining and a line was thrown to him and he was dragged to safety. Of the six men on board, three were drowned and one dead and two living were brought to shore.

25. A Cliff Rescue, 1874

November and December 1874 brought the worst storm and the highest seas to Seaham that could be remembered in thirty-seven years. On the morning of Sunday 29 November a small Wells schooner, *Mary Ann*, loaded with wheat, was making for Seaham Harbour. Those watching from land could see that she was in a disabled state and unmanageable. She was driven by the heavy seas behind the north pier with waves washing over her with tremendous force. It was obvious that the crew, who had lashed themselves to the rigging, were in dire straits. The crew of the lifeboat were assembled but they knew it would be useless to attempt a rescue in their boat as

The lifeboat Good Templar *which was stationed at Sunderland from 1873-76 at Roker No 1 Station and was instrumental in saving fourteen lives.* Author's collection

she would be dashed to pieces against the pier and the rocks. Lines were thrown and by this means three of the crew were dragged through the water and up the side of the pier, battered and bruised, but safe. The master, Ransom, was the last man aboard the stricken ship and, although lines were thrown, he did not attempt to use them. John Marshall, a pilot, tried to reach Ransom but, before he could do so, the part of the rigging that the master was lashed to gave way and fell into the sea. Ransom's body was found on the beach the following afternoon.

On Tuesday 8 December a Faversham vessel, *Queen of the Isles*, sailing from Boulogne to Shields was seen driving towards shore opposite Watson and Ripling's Chemical Works. The lifeboat was prepared under the command of the coxswain, John Marshall, but it was quickly established that the lifeboat would be useless on this occasion because of the situation of the ship. The Chief Officer of the coastguards, Mr Ching, assembled his men on the beach with the rocket apparatus at the ready. Immediately the vessel struck ground the rocket lines were fired and, with difficulty, Captain Dyson and his crew of seven were brought to safety before the ship became a total wreck. About two hours later a Whitby vessel, *Conqueror*, sailing from Ramsgate to Sunderland, was seen to be coming ashore. This time the rescue was more difficult as the men and rocket apparatus had to be lowered down the cliffs on ropes. Within minutes of the vessel striking the rocks the coastguards, lifeboat crew and volunteers were at work. Captain Crooke and his crew of seven were all brought off safely. This ship also became a total wreck. The rescuers kept watch all through the following day until the storm abated but, thankfully, their services were not required again.

26. Breeches Buoy, 1880

The final days of October 1880 saw severe weather which affected all of Europe and the British Isles. Wednesday 27 October dawned with strong gales, lashing winds and heavy seas which increased in severity over the following two days. Seaham Harbour saw its first casualty at about 4 pm when a vessel was seen to be drifting onshore. It was a Faversham brig, *British Ensign*, which had been sailing from Ramsgate to Shields. The Volunteer Life Brigade was quickly assembled and ready with their rocket apparatus. Seven men could be seen clinging to the rigging as the ship took to the beach. It took a few efforts but eventually communication was established with the line and six men were brought to safety by breeches buoy. A young apprentice, Edward Packman, somehow slipped out of the cradle and was drowned.

A postcard, c1903, depicting the Sunderland south outlet, fish quay and lifeboat, possibly the Richard and Nellie Hodges *which was in service from 1894-1908 and was instrumental in saving eight lives.* George Nairn

Shortly afterwards another vessel came ashore between Ryhope and Seaham. She was a Colchester brigantine, *Zosteria*, which had been sailing from her home port to Sunderland. Captain Pullen and his crew of five were utterly exhausted so great difficulty was experienced getting them to safety. Although the vessel was only thirty yards (approx 27m) from land, the breakers were huge. Some of the coastguards were almost up to their necks in the sea. As two of the men were being pulled in by hawser they fell from the buoy. One man managed to seize the rope and by this means was hauled to safety but the other was not so lucky and he went down just out of reach of the rescuers.

About noon on Thursday a schooner was seen drifting ashore near the new gasworks at Hendon. Her sails were in tatters and she was at the mercy of the wind and sea. She came ashore just near the entrance to the River Wear in a position which could be reached by rocket lines. Her crew were in the rigging and, while the rocket apparatus was being got ready, tremendous waves could be seen washing over the vessel's deck. The rockets were fired and the lines were quickly secured by the crew of the schooner. One of the crew was just a young lad and it took some persuasion for him to utilize his chance of escape. When he was eventually brought to shore it was found he was very weak and utterly exhausted. The vessel was the *Huntley* of Faversham, which had been sailing from Gravesend to the Tyne when she was caught in the storm. Captain W Gray and his crew of five were all brought to safety.

At the same time the crew of the *Huntley* were being assisted another vessel had come ashore at Ryhope. She was a Colchester brigantine, *Zosteria*, which had been sailing from her home port to Sunderland. A number of men on land had been watching as the vessel was driven ashore and, using hand lines, they managed to drag the crew of five to safety. Captain H P Pullen declined, at first, to leave the vessel in the hope that she could be floated at high tide. He eventually must have realised that he was in a dangerous position and he then agreed to be hauled to land. The vessel later became a total wreck.

Later that evening a Portsmouth schooner, *Henry and Elizabeth*, came ashore at the foot of Ryhope Dene. Three of her crew came ashore in their small ship's boat. The remaining three were brought ashore by a local man, Henry Wilson, wading out through the surf and throwing them a line.

Just after 10 pm on Friday guns were fired from the Brigade House to inform the members of the Life Brigade that a vessel had been seen off Ryhope burning flares. The apparatus was taken by carriage to the shore opposite to where the ship was at anchor. She was too far out for the rocket lines to be of any use and also it appeared that the flares were for a tug to take her into port. As there was a danger of the vessel stranding, the Brigade men stood by but their services were not required. A steam-tug, *Rescue*, went out to the vessel and towed her safely into port. The vessel was a Shoreham brig, *Rapid*, and her captain stated later that he had never seen such a gale in all his twenty years at sea. When the *Rescue* was going to the aid of the *Rapid*, on passing the Hendon buoys the tug-master saw a vessel anchored but floating bottom up with no sign of her crew.

✦ ～✦✦✦✦✦ ✦

27. The Fate of the *Aurora*, 1885

The *Aurora* was an iron screw-steamer built at Middlesbrough by Raylton, Dixon and Co. in 1883. She was 264 feet (80,4672m) in length, thirty-six feet breadth and had a gross tonnage of 1,717.50. Her engines had been supplied and fitted by Richardson and Son of Hartlepool and her managing owner was Richard J Blacklin of Church Street, West Hartlepool.

The lifeboat Nancy Newbon *which was stationed at Sunderland from 1908-12 at No 4 Station and was instrumental in saving nine lives.* Author's collection

The *Aurora* had left London on 22 November 1885 bound for Savannah with a cargo of super-phosphates. F F Ormandy, of Sunderland, was the master of twenty-two crew and, at the end of her voyage, the ship was found to have also been carrying two stowaways who had boarded at London. She had entered Hartlepool Dock to take on about 700 tons of bunker-coal and some repairs were carried out on her engines before she left on the afternoon of Wednesday 25 November.

A pilot, George Davison, was taken on board to guide the ship out from Union Dock. When the *Aurora* reached the head of Middleton Pier he left the vessel as the seas were running too heavy for his coble. If he had not left when he did he would have had to have stayed aboard until the ship had docked further up the coast.

The *Aurora* was in tow of the steam-tug, *Blanche*, with another tug astern to steady her but after leaving the piers she went too far to port. The master of the tug called to the crew to pull their vessel astern but they did not appear to hear the instruction. She seemed to be going at full speed still continuing too far south. The tug went hard to starboard to try and straighten the *Aurora* but the tow-line broke. She was heading for the Longscar and the tug-master again shouted, this time his instructions were heeded and the crew pulled their vessel to starboard. The tug-master thought it was now safe to leave the *Aurora* to make her own way. Unbeknown to the crew, however, the ship had struck the rocks and sprung a leak. They had felt her jar quite heavily two or three times but did not realise that any damage had been caused. A short time later it was realised the vessel was taking on water so the pumps were manned. There was a gale blowing and the seas were high but the master decided it would be too dangerous to try and turn his ship in the channel to make it back into Hartlepool so he would run for the Tyne instead. After the crew had been pumping for nearly two hours and trying to bung the holes where the water was coming in, it was decided their efforts were fruitless and they should abandon ship. By this time they were offshore from Seaham. The ship's three small boats were lowered at about 8 pm with the crew dividing themselves amongst them.

When daylight broke on Thursday morning two of the *Aurora's* small boats were seen just south of Seaham Harbour and an alarm was raised. The coastguard station immediately readied the life-saving apparatus and the *Sisters Carter of Harrogate* lifeboat was manned and launched with a crew consisting of

A postcard depicting Robert Robinson a member of the Sunderland Voluntary Life Brigade. George Nairn

coxswain John Marshall, Frederick Quilter, Morley Scott, John Bruce, Adam Colley, W Hook, W Reed, D Wallace, R Morse, John Scott, George Scott, George Neil, John Rogers and David Mead. There was an immense sea and, although every effort was made by the crew of the lifeboat, they could not get out of the harbour. More men boarded her, so she was almost double-banked with crew, and another attempt was made. This time the lifeboat managed to get outside the piers but the sea was so strong that once again she was washed back in and the crew had no choice but to abandon their efforts. Meanwhile, the two small boats, one flying a small signal of distress, were being tossed about like matchsticks. One was then seen to be slowly washed towards land and she eventually went ashore a little to the north of Seaham Dene. A crowd of people made there way to the spot and hauled the boat with its exhausted crew to shore. There were nine men aboard, of which four, suffering from exposure and exhaustion, were taken to the infirmary. A second boat came ashore near Ryhope Dean which had left the *Aurora* with six men aboard including the master, who had been the last to leave the ship. Sometime through the night this boat had capsized and two of the occupants, John Burdon and August Nestram, were drowned and another, H Gibson, died shortly after reaching safety.

There were fears that the third boat, carrying eight men, was lost but word arrived at Seaham later in the day that they had come ashore at Hawthorn Dene. These men had been trying to reach land for twelve hours and were utterly exhausted. They were being watched from the cliffs by a coastguard, Walters, and a commissioned boatman, Hill, who tried to direct them by signals to a safe place to land. Unfortunately, their boat beached at the base of steep cliffs. Walters and Hill climbed down the cliff and led the men through the surf until they came to a spot where the rocks could be scaled by the exhausted crew. With a great deal of assistance from their two rescuers the shipwrecked men managed to pull themselves up by holding onto tufts of grass and crevices in the rocks until they reached the fields above where R L Pemberton junior, of Hawthorn Tower, and others were waiting to give help. The men were taken to Mr Nixon's farm at Easington. The black steward, George Moses Johnson, had suffered from the ordeal more severely than his shipmates and, although eventually brought to safety, he died shortly afterwards.

A Board of Trade inquiry was held into the circumstances of the loss of the *Aurora*. The captain blamed the pilot for not staying aboard and the pilot blamed the captain saying that he had told him it was unsafe to leave port. The end result was that the managing owner, Mr Blackin, was found responsible as the captain took his orders from him. It was in the owner's hands to decide whether it was safe for their ship to leave port. Partial blame was also laid on the pilot and the captain, the former for leaving the ship too early and the latter for allowing him to do so.

A report at the time told a tale of human selfishness. A well-wisher had purchased a bottle of brandy to be taken to the shipwrecked men to help with their revival. The brandy was entrusted to a sailor to be delivered to those that needed it but instead of delivering the gift to its proper recipients he hid himself out of the way and consumed the entire contents of the bottle. The sailor was found insensible and was arrested. His stomach was pumped so that he was fit to appear in the Magistrates' Court where he was then prosecuted for theft.

28. A New Century, 1901

The end of the first year of the twentieth century once again brought disaster to shipping and life up and down the North East coast. On Tuesday, 12 November 1901 a large French iron full-rigged ship, *Quillota*, sailing from Nantes to North Shields under the command of

Captain C Delepine had been making for the Tyne when she was seen being driven south in winds ENE and a force 10 gale. She hit the Hendon Rocks in the early hours of Wednesday morning. Her distress flares were seen burning but she was too far from land for rocket lines to reach and no small boat could have survived the huge seas. A search party went along the shores in search of survivors and two men were found embedded in the clay on the bank. They were dug out but one was already dead and the other died of exposure and exhaustion a few minutes after being freed. He had no form of identification on his person. Captain Delepine and four of the crew had managed to reach land. With no shoes and their clothes soaking wet they had wandered along the beach until they found a slope in the embankment that they could climb. Another man, Lienel Francole, was found wandering along the road soaking wet and disorientated. He later said that he had been washed overboard, luckily wearing a lifebelt, and had swum until he reached solid ground. The survivors were taken to Hendon to be cared for and all eventually recovered. The vessel had been carrying a crew of twenty-two and one passenger of which seventeen had drowned.

When the gale was at its height the seas were so high over the Sunderland piers that they were completely obliterated beneath the rolling surf. A Goole schooner, *Harriot*, tried to enter the harbour but the crew could not control their craft against the elements. Their vessel was driven into the shore behind the North Eastern Marine Engineering works. The captain, Frederick Bayley, and a seaman, Thomas Flint were saved but Percy Blake, the mate, and Frederick Gill, who was only nineteen, were drowned.

Later in the day a small ketch barge, *Europa*, tried to make the harbour. She had sailed from Margate and had been caught in the storm near to the Tees where her rigging had been damaged. By the time she reached Sunderland her rigging was gone and her crew could not bring her in. She drifted helplessly in a crab-like fashion until she hit the end of the south pier. Of the crew of five on board two managed to jump onto the pier and one was rescued by means of a line. James Cook, the captain and a seaman, William Plowman, tried to jump onto the pier but the vessel shifted and they both fell into the sea and were swept away.

A Folkestone snow, *Cambois*, with a crew of seven under Captain Harrison, was in tow of a tug offshore from Whitburn when the tow-rope broke and she drove onto Rockley Way Rocks with tremendous force and immediately began to break up. A practice had been due to take place by the Volunteer Life Brigade at Whitburn so the apparatus was at the ready and no time was lost in attending the emergency. Two attempts with the lines were fruitless but on the third try the line hit

An engraving from 1832 showing the use of Dennett's Rocket lines. Author's collection

its mark. The crew of the *Cambois* attached the line to the mainmast but they did not know how to handle the apparatus so instead of a rescue a tragedy followed. Three of the men were swept from the deck by the huge waves and three jumped into the sea. Two men were seen clinging to the side of the vessel and were not seen again. Three of the Life Brigade men, Ranson, Brown and Young, waded through the surf with a line attached to them to assist the exhausted crew. Six men were helped to shore but two of them died soon after.

Other vessels that suffered at the fury of the storm that day were a Portsmouth schooner, *Alcor*, which was carrying a cargo of coal from Sunderland to Whitstable with Captain Altensel and his crew of five. Three men were lost when she was wrecked at Noses Point at Seaham. A Swedish schooner, *Sirius*, with a crew of seven under Captain Jons Petersson, was stranded near to Hawthorn beach. The crew remained on their vessel until low tide when they were got off safely. A small London schooner, *Miss Thomas*, was driven ashore near Hawthorn Hive. Captain Hitchens and his crew of four were got off safely.

The following day a Plymouth barquentine, *Lile*, was carrying a cargo of coal from Sunderland to Malpas when she foundered near Sunderland. Captain J Pope and his crew of five were lost.

The final disaster that year for Sunderland was towards the end of

December. A schooner was observed just off the River Wear burning flares of distress. Driven before the strong winds, while she was trying to make for the harbour, she struck the south pier. The vessel broke up almost immediately and wreckage was washed up on the beach behind the North East Engineering Company's works. The Sunderland Volunteer Life Brigade, when they were informed of the event, began a search for survivors but found nothing. Their spokesman later stated that, even if they had known earlier that the ship was in trouble, due to its position, it was doubtful that they could have been of any assistance. It later transpired that the vessel had been a Teignmouth three-masted schooner, *Eliza Bain*, sailing from her home port to Sunderland carrying a cargo of china clay. There had been five men aboard her when she was wrecked.

29. Gallantry Medals

1856: Silver Medal to Joseph Hodgson, a carver, in twelve years of service, for personally saving ten people from drowning and assisting, in lifeboats and other boats, the rescue of about seventeen others.

1858: Silver Medal to coxswain W Davison for long service.

1874: Silver Medal to John Marshall junior for his gallant, but unsuccessful attempt to save the master of the Wells schooner *Lady Ann* when she was wrecked against the north pier of Seaham Harbour in 1870.

1891: Silver Medal to coxswain R Thompson, for general services.

Part III

Shields, Tynemouth and Cullercoats

The Tyne was a busy harbour in the eighteenth century but was extremely exposed to the ravages of the sea. The Herd Sand was hazardous to shipping trying to enter the river from the south and the Black Middens Rocks from the north. When the River Tyne Improvement Act was passed in Parliament in 1850 work began on two huge stone piers at the entrance to the river to improve safety for shipping but there were still many casualties as the piers and breakwaters were not completed until 1910. By that time ships that relied on sail alone had been almost relegated to the past.

In 1786 Lionel Lukin, a prominent London coachbuilder, had converted a coble into a boat to be used for saving life. This boat was stationed at Bamburgh. In March 1789 the *Adventurer* of Newcastle struck the Herd Sand in front of hundreds of spectators who could only stand and watch helplessly as the crew fell from the rigging and were drowned. It is believed that this tragic incident prompted a group of businessmen and ship-owners of Tynemouth to organise a lifeboat

A postcard depicting the No 2 Station lifeboat Forester *stationed at Shields. Two lifeboats of this name were in service, one from 1872-1900 and the second from 1900-05.* Author's collection

A postcard depicting the lifeboat Tyne *on display at South Shields. The* Tyne *was built in 1833 and performed her last rescue in 1882 after being instrumental in saving over 1020 lives. She was presented to the South Shields Corporation in 1894. The* Tyne *is the second oldest preserved lifeboat in the world.* Author's collection

for the area. An advertisement was placed in the *Newcastle Courant* offering a prize of two guineas (£2.10) for the best design to be put forward for a boat with the capabilities to render assistance when life was in danger. Two men's designs were considered suitable for the purpose, William Wouldhave and Henry Greathead. The first boat, *Original,* was built by Henry Greathead, incorporating the designs of both men. She was launched in 1789 and was the first purpose-built lifeboat in the world. The *Original* was stationed at South Shields and looked after by the Tyne Lifeboat Institution which later became the Tyne Lifeboat Society. The boat was manned by the Tyne pilots and was in service until January 1830 when, going to the aid of the *Glatton* from South Shields, she was driven onto the rocks where she broke in two and two of her crew lost their lives. A second boat, donated by the Duke of Northumberland in 1798, and also built by Henry Greathead, was the *Northumberland* and was stationed at the Low Lights. The present boat, *Northumberland Spirit,* launched in 2000, was named in memory of this second boat. The *Tyne* was built in 1833 by Oliver and Sons of South Shields and presented by Thomas Forrest, a South Shields ship-owner. She was in service until 1882. The *Providence* was built in 1842 and she and the *Tyne* were stationed at the Coble

Landing, South Shields. The *Providence,* whilst going to the rescue of the brig *Betsy* in December 1849, capsized and twenty-five of her crew were drowned. The *Tyne* was launched but only managed to save four of the lifeboat crew and the crew of the brig. In 1894 the *Tyne* was given to the South Shields Corporation and, although she was badly damaged when she was bombed in 1941, restoration was carried out and she remains on show to the present day alongside a memorial to William Wouldhave and Henry Greathead.

The Tynemouth Lifeboat Institution remained independent until 1862, when the RNLI established a station at Prior s Haven and in 1865 No 2 Station was put in place at the Black Middens. Two more lifeboats were then in service, the *Prior,* stationed on the Herd Sand and the *Constance,* a gift from GJ Fenwick of Seaton Sluice, stationed at Prior s Haven. In 1872 it was decided that a larger lifeboat was required at the No 2 Station and so the *Forester* was built. She was a gift from the funds of the Ancient Order of Foresters. In 1900 a second *Forester* was provided from the same Institution. In 1905 the second *Forester* was withdrawn and No 2 Station closed.

At the end of 1874 the *Constance* was out on service to the SS *Breeze* of Hartlepool when she struck some floating wreckage. She made it safely back to shore but was so badly damaged it was decided not to be worth the repair. The crew of the *Breeze* were taken off by the lifeboat *Northumberland.* The *Constance* was replaced in 1875 by the *Charles Dibdin,* provided by the Civil Service Lifeboat Fund of which

The first launch of the lifeboat Co-operator No.1 *at Cullercoats in 1884. She was presented by the Manchester Central Co-operative Board and did service until 1907 during which time she was instrumental in saving twenty eight lives.*
Author's collection

An engraving of shipwrecks on the rocks at Tynemouth in the nineteenth century.
Author's collection

Charles Dibdin was the Honorary Secretary. In 1904 this boat was replaced with the *J McConnell Hussey*, which had been built in 1893 but converted to give service as a motor lifeboat before being stationed at Tynemouth. Prior's Haven Station was closed in 1904 and the motor lifeboat left at moorings.

The *Henry Vernon*, built in 1905, was one of the first RNLI experimental lifeboats built with an engine fitted in. Provided out of a legacy from Arabella Vernon of Weston-Super-Mare, she was stationed at Tynemouth and placed under the command of Lieutenant H E Burton, later to become Major Burton. This lifeboat was to prove its worth when the crew rescued fifty people from the hospital ship, HMHS *Rohilla*, which went aground at Saltwick Nab near Whitby on 1 November 1914. After initial rescues by the Whitby lifeboats it was decided that a motor lifeboat was the only possible way to save the remaining survivors still on board the wrecked ship. A telegram was sent to Tynemouth requesting their aid. The lifeboat crew took a quantity of oil with them and this was used to flatten the waves so they could get close enough to perform the rescue. Of the 229 people aboard the *Rohilla*, sixty-two crew and twenty-eight passengers lost their lives.

In 1848 a coble manned by seven local Cullercoats men was in the act of taking a pilot out to a ship when it capsized and all aboard were drowned. The Duke of Northumberland owned much of the land in

An engraving of ships leaving the mouth of the Tyne in the nineteenth century.
Author's collection

Cullercoats and he would have been personally involved with many of the local people. The tragedy affected him deeply and prompted him to provide funds for an RNLI station at Cullercoats. After the tragedy in 1849 of the South Shields lifeboat *Providence*, when twenty of her crew of twenty-four were drowned when the boat capsized, he offered a prize for a new, safer design of a self-righting lifeboat. James Beeching of Great Yarmouth won the competition but the RNLI employed James Peake, Master Shipwright of the Royal Naval Dock at Woolwich, to modify and make improvements to the submitted design. This first self-righting boat, *Percy*, was delivered to Cullercoats in 1852 after numerous sea-trials. The boathouse was also built at the Duke's expense. The *Percy* was used to escort local fishermen during bad weather and also to aid in rescues from larger ships that were in danger around the nearby coast. In 1859 the *Percy* was found to have dry rot so was replaced with a boat of the same name also paid for by the Duke of Northumberland. She was replaced in 1866 by the *Palmerston* which was donated by Peter Reid of the London Stock Exchange. In 1884 the Co-operative Wholesale Society presented Cullercoats RNLI with the *Co-operator No 1* which remained in service until 1907 when it was replaced by a boat of the same name by the same donors. The second *Co-operator No 1* was in service until 1937.

30. A Disgraceful Scene, 1852

The last three months of 1852 brought severe weather to the coast making it extremely hazardous for shipping. On Wednesday 27 October a King's Lynn brig, *Unity*, was driven onto the Herd Sand. Captain Massingham and the crew of six were taken off by the lifeboat.

Late on the night of Thursday 28 October a Norwegian barque, *Marie Elizabeth*, was driven onshore on the Herd Sand. She had been sailing from London to her home port, Christiana, with a general cargo. On Tuesday, 26 October, nine days into her journey and just off the Dogger Bank, she sprung a leak. As her hold was fast filling with water and the ship was in danger of sinking, her captain, H Parvels, had hailed a passing vessel, *Woodbine*, to take his crew on board. A small boat was lowered from the barque with three men and a boy in her. One man and the boy were taken aboard the *Woodbine* and the remaining two men returned to the *Marie Elizabeth* to collect a further three crewmen. As the small boat with its five men began its second trip a large wave hit the small boat and capsized her, throwing the men into the sea. The barque's long-boat was launched but this too capsized as soon as it struck the water. The *Woodbine* tried to get near enough the distressed vessel for the men to jump onto her deck but could not do so. Captain Parvels signalled to Captain Davis of the *Woodbine* that

A sketch from the Illustrated London News *depicting the salvage of ships aground at Tynemouth in 1850.* Author's collection

he would try to get his disabled vessel to shore. The remainder of the crew kept working the pumps and the *Marie Elizabeth* limped towards the Tyne but, before she could make it into the harbour, she struck on the Herd Sand and began immediately to break up. The captain and the five men still aboard were rescued by the South Shields lifeboat. One of the men, a fisherman from Greenland who was a passenger, had been jammed and crushed when the barque hit the rocks and he died soon after the rescue. Two of the five that were washed out of the small boat were picked up out at sea. All told, of the thirteen aboard, four lost their lives.

In what was later described as a barbarous and disgraceful scene a number of local people, both men and women, rushed to the spot with axes and began breaking open casks of wine that had been amongst the cargo. They shaped their waterproof jackets into sacks and even used their boots to fill with wine to carry triumphantly to shore. Some had tools with which they bored into the casks and drank the port and wine from the holes they had made. Lying drunk and insensible at the water's edge they had to be dragged to safety or would have been drowned. Some were taken to the workhouse to sleep it off. A few were in such a state that it was thought they may never awaken. People were also picking up bales of raw cotton, umbrellas, silk, lace and anything that looked to be of any value. Three customs men were soon on the scene but only managed to save a portion of what was scattered near the shore. They were not a large enough force to stop so many pilferers. Luckily for the owners much of the cargo was still on the wreck and was later salvaged. Some of those that were caught stealing the cargo were later fined between £1 and £10 at North and South Shields Magistrates' Courts under the Wreckers and Salvage Act.

On the same day as the *Marie Elizabeth* was wrecked, a Wisbech brig, *Union*, was also driven onto the Herd Sand with Captain Fox and a crew of seven being rescued by the South Shield's lifeboat. A French brig, *Hypolite Marie*, and a London schooner, *Ormsby Hall*, also drove ashore at the same place. The following day a Clay brig, *Lively*, met the same fate.

On Sunday 12 December a Shields barque, *Jane and Elizabeth*, broke her moorings due to the strong tide in the river. She struck the stones at the Bar and rolled over onto her beam ends drowning two of her crew of thirteen. A screw-steamer, *William and Mary*, sunk after striking the wreck of the *Jane and Elizabeth*. Two barques, *Countess of Durham* and *Edward Cohen* were driven onto the Herd Sand the same day.

31. Nine on the Rocks, 1853-4

The end of 1853 and the beginning of 1854 brought storms which matched the fury of those that had swept the North East coast in October of 1852. In mid-December of 1853 a Shields brig, *Sylph*, after her captain refusing the services of a steam-tug, was driven onto the Black Middens. Her crew were rescued by the South Shields lifeboat. The lifeboat gave service in another rescue towards the end of that month when a snow, *Cygnet*, sailing from London to Shields, was wrecked on the Herd Sand.

The first two days of 1854 heralded severe weather but by the morning of Tuesday 3 January, although still not ideal, the wind had moderated slightly so the masters of several vessels decided to put to sea. By nightfall the wind had started to gust heavily again and on Wednesday morning a large fleet of ships were heading for the safety of the Tyne, amongst them many that had set sail from there the previous day. A number reached safe harbour with no trouble but seven were driven across the bar and onto the rocks where rocket lines and lifeboats were used to bring all the crews to safety.

At about 11am a small schooner was seen heading for the Tyne. Although she was not showing signals of distress, it was clear to those

A sketch from the Illustrated London News *of the* Royal Adelaide *battling against the storm. This vessel was sailing from Cork to London when she was caught in a storm and wrecked on Tynemouth rocks in April 1850.* Author's collection

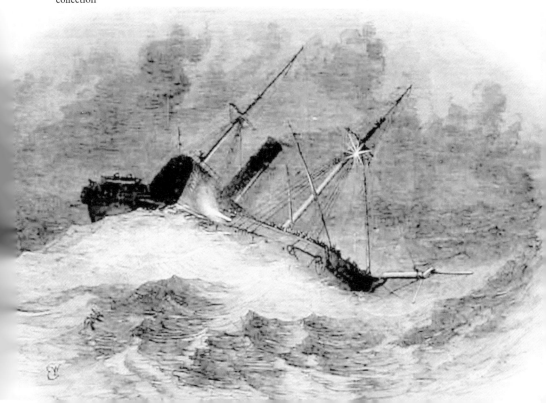

A sketch from the Illustrated London News *of the remains of the* Royal Adelaide *after she was wrecked at Tynemouth.* Author's collection

observing from the shore that she was in trouble as she was listing, probably because her ballast had shifted, and was heading for the rocks. Five men were seen clinging to the rigging and one to the crosstrees as she struck and went over on her beam ends. The waves pounded the disabled ship and she lurched causing the top masts to give way and the man who had been clinging to the crosstrees to fall. As he fell his leg became entangled in the ropes and he was thrown head downward and killed. With every sway of the vessel the man's body, still caught by his leg, could be seen swinging with the motion. The vessel was only a hundred yards from shore but the position was such that a rocket line could not reach the remaining crew. There was no lifeboat available but even if there had been it was doubtful whether it could have reached the stricken vessel. The schooner remained in its precarious position for a little less than half an hour with the remainder of the crew clinging to the rigging but they could be seen to be becoming weaker by the minute. A wave then hit with tremendous force and turned the vessel bottom up and the men were gone. Amongst the debris that floated ashore were the ship's papers which showed the wrecked vessel had been the *Eliza* of Kirkwall under the command of Walter Scott. Later that night another schooner went on the rocks with her crew being rescued by the South Shields lifeboat. By the following day, of the nine ships that had gone onto the rocks, all but two were total wrecks. The severe weather continued until the middle of January and other vessels were wrecked and stranded, both on the Herd Sand and the Black Middens. These included three Shields vessels, *Anns*, *Elizabeth* and *Antelope*, a Sunderland snow, *New Messenger*, the *Eweretta* of Hull, *Amphitrite* of London, *Arethusa* of Blyth, *Rebecca and Elizabeth* of Falmouth, *Hannah* of Arbroath, *Junius* of Norway and *James and Ann* of Ipswich. Some of these crews were taken off with the use of rocket apparatus and some by lifeboat. Sixty-five men from the wrecked vessels were given assistance by the Shipwrecked Mariners Royal Benevolent Society to return to their home ports.

Although the river police kept a close eye on the ship's cargoes there were still wreckers about. At least fourteen men were taken before the magistrates at South Shields and their punishments varied from twenty-one days in gaol to fines of £1 and upward.

32. The Herd Sand, 1857

On the morning of Sunday, 4 January 1857 some fishermen noticed a schooner that seemed to be in great distress about a mile to the east of Cullercoats. They could see no sign of any crew and as the sea was washing over the deck it had to be assumed that the men had been washed overboard. As the fishermen watched, the schooner sank beneath the waves. Later that morning wreckage was washed ashore and an oar was found bearing an inscription of the name *Reform*. A wrecked boat, *Alma*, came ashore with no sign of the crew and also a mainsail assumed to be from another vessel that had been taken by the sea.

About 10 am a light brig was seen to the north of Tynemouth Castle with her main-top sail split. Shortly after she took the bar to the south where a heavy sea struck her and laid her broadside. The brig, which was the *Sarah Helen* of London, stayed in that position for a few minutes and then righted herself but the mainmast was gone and she was driven over the Herd Sand. The three Shields lifeboats were quickly manned and launched and they succeeded in taking off Captain Rievelly and all but one of the crew. A young apprentice, Alexander Cox, had been washed overboard when the ship had gone broadside.

A few minutes later a French lugger attempted to take the bar but she was driven onto the Herd Sand. The crew climbed onto the rigging where it seemed as though they were in a perilous position with the breakers washing over the vessel. One of the lifeboats went alongside but the master had told his men that if they left the ship he would knock their heads off. The lugger was driven a long way up the beach

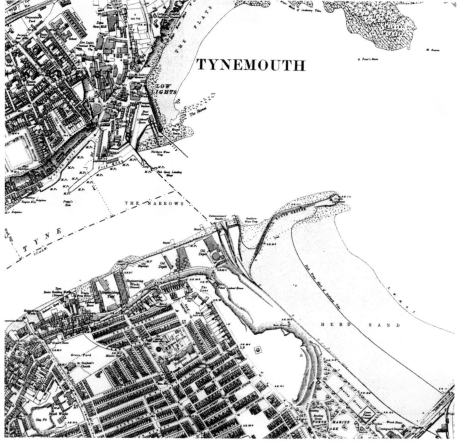

The mouth of the Tyne showing the position of the Herd Sand to the south and the rocks to the north. Ordnance Survey, Mouth of the Tyne, 1898

and a little later the master and crew got themselves off safely. Two of the lifeboats then took off the crew of another schooner that went onto the Herd Sand. Six of the lifeboat's oars were broken in this rescue.

During this storm it was said that at least fifteen vessels had been seen, either by shore lookouts or those at sea, to have foundered with all crew. Between Berwick and Yarmouth more than sixty vessels had stranded and many of them had been pounded into fragments during the worst of the weather.

33. *Lovely Nelly*, 1861

On the morning of Thursday 1 January 1861, during a severe ESE gale bringing with it sleet and snow, a Seaham brig, *Lovely Nelly*, was sighted from the Spanish Battery showing a signal of distress and being swept by the heavy seas towards the coastline. The rocket apparatus team was quickly assembled and headed along the coast towards Whitley Bay followed by many of the local people. The onlookers could see that, with some of her sails gone, the vessel was becoming more unmanageable with each passing minute. The crew of the brig were exhausted and, deciding their efforts to sail northwards were fruitless, ran their vessel ashore on Whitley Sand, about five miles north of Shields. They were about three-quarters of a mile from shore which was too far for the rocket lines to reach.

The Cullercoats lifeboat, *Percy*, was taken out of her boathouse and six horses harnessed to her carriage. Local men and woman helped to drag and push the boat over the sand to Brier Dene where she was launched with a crew consisting of John Redford (coxswain), John Taylor (second coxswain), John Chisholm, William Dodds, William Harrison, Thomas Mills, Joseph Robinson, John Smith, Barty and Robert Taylor, Robert Francis, William Storey, George Smith and William Stocks.

Despite the heavy seas the lifeboat was manoeuvred alongside the stricken vessel and a grapnel was thrown aboard and secured. Six men released their grip on the rigging and slowly made their way towards the lifeboat via the grapnel line. Three were taken aboard the lifeboat but the other three were swept into the sea by the huge waves washing over the deck. One by one these three were hauled to safety by the strong, willing hands of the lifeboat crew. Only one of the crew now remained in peril was the twelve-year-old cabin boy, Thomas Thompson of Seaham. He clung to the rigging, his face bloody from a

A postcard dating from the early twentieth century depicting the two piers and lighthouses at the entrance to Shields. Author's collection

A Lawson steam-tug pulling a large five masted sailing vessel up the Tyne in the early part of the twentieth century. Author's collection

An old postcard depicting a stormy sea lashing the pier and lighthouse at Tynemouth. Author's collection

cut to his head, as the *Lovely Nelly* began to go to pieces beneath him. The lifeboat crew shouted to him to jump into the lifeboat but, frozen in his fear, the boy did not move. Redford saw that the main-mast was ready to fall and knew if he waited any longer he would be placing the lives of the men in his boat in jeopardy. He shouted the order to cut the rope, which was immediately done. As the lifeboat moved clear of the doomed vessel the main-mast fell entangling the boy in the mass of ropes before sweeping him into the sea. The lifeboat crew made a desperate attempt to reach the boy but he disappeared out of sight beneath the waves. His body was later recovered and given to his family for burial.

Those that were rescued were Captain Henry Stainbridge, George Kirby (the mate), Henry Watson, John Walton, Robin Bond and John Adamson.

On the afternoon of Friday 8 February 1861 the weather was calm when around 100 vessels left the Tyne, most of them fully laden with a cargo of coal. Later that day a storm warning was issued up and down the North-East coast which gave cause for concern, and rightly so, as that weekend saw the coastguards, pilots and lifeboat crews stretched to their utter limit.

Many of the ships that left the port realised their peril and turned back for the safety of the Tyne but some were too late to outrun the strong north easterly winds. The havoc that this particular storm wreaked began at about midnight when the South Shields pilots saw the *Minerva* of Whitby coming from the south and in obvious danger of hitting the foundation stones at the end of the south pier. The lifeboat *Providence* was launched and, with a tremendous struggle, managed to reach the vessel. A line with a grapnel hook was thrown onto the vessel but in the darkness, instead of landing on the deck, the hook caught one of the crew in the face and caused a serious injury. A young apprentice, John Storm, fell overboard when he tried to jump into the lifeboat. A line was thrown and he managed to hold onto it until he could be dragged to safety. Unfortunately, as the lifeboat came near enough for a rescue, it hit the side of the *Minerva* nipping one of the boy's legs in the process. All nine of the crew were rescued and Storm was taken to Newcastle infirmary suffering a broken leg. A short time later the *Sarah Ann* from North Shields was seen to be in a critical position on the Herd Sand. The second lifeboat, *Tyne*, was launched and, once again, the crew were successfully brought to safety. The *Sarah Ann* was washed up onto the beach and stranded. Shortly before 7 am a schooner, *Fowlis* of Inverness, struck the rocks at the same place the *Minerva* had gone to pieces only a few hours previously. The *Providence* was launched but their attempts to approach the vessel were thwarted by the huge stones that threatened to stave in the lifeboat.

TREATMENT OF THE APPARENTLY DROWNED.

ROYAL NATIONAL LIFE-BOAT INSTITUTION.

Incorporated by Royal Charter.—Supported by Voluntary Contributions.

PATRONESS—HER MOST GRACIOUS MAJESTY THE QUEEN.

DIRECTIONS FOR RESTORING THE APPARENTLY DROWNED.

THE leading principles of the following Directions for the Restoration of the apparently Dead from Drowning are founded on those of the late DR. MARSHALL HALL, combined with those of DR. H. R. SILVESTER, and are the result of extensive inquiries which were made by the Institution in 1863-4 amongst Medical Men, Medical Bodies, and Coroners throughout the United Kingdom. These Directions have been extensively circulated by the INSTITUTION throughout the United Kingdom and in the Colonies. They are also in use in Her Majesty's Fleet, in the Coastguard Service, and at all the Stations of the British Army at home and abroad.

I.

SEND immediately for medical assistance, blankets, and dry clothing, but proceed to treat the Patient *instantly* on the spot, in the open air, with the face downward, whether on shore or afloat; exposing the face, neck, and chest to the wind, except in severe weather, and removing all tight clothing from the neck and chest, especially the braces.

The points to be aimed at are—first and *immediately*, the RESTORATION OF BREATHING; and secondly, after breathing is restored, the PROMOTION OF WARMTH AND CIRCULATION.

The efforts to *restore Breathing* must be commenced immediately and energetically, and persevered in for one or two hours, or until a medical man has pronounced that life is extinct. Efforts to promote *Warmth* and *Circulation*, beyond removing the wet clothes and drying the skin, must not be made until the first appearance of natural breathing : for if circulation of the blood be induced before breathing has recommenced, the restoration to life will be endangered.

II.—TO RESTORE BREATHING.

To CLEAR THE THROAT.—Place the patient on the floor or ground with the face downwards, and one of the arms under the forehead, in which position all fluids will more readily escape by the mouth, and the tongue itself will fall forward, leaving the entrance into the windpipe free. Assist this operation by wiping and cleansing the mouth.

If satisfactory breathing commences, use the treatment described below to promote Warmth.

If there be only slight breathing—or no breathing—or if the breathing fail, then—

To EXCITE BREATHING—Turn the patient well and instantly on the side, supporting the head, and

1.—INSPIRATION.

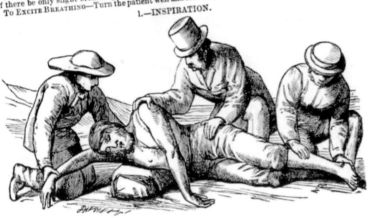

Front page of a pocket leaflet on the treatment of an apparently drowned person. These leaflets were distributed by the RNLI in 1865 to all their lifeboat crews.
Author's collection

The lifeboat crew landed and tried to launch the lifeboat stationed at the Laws but could not get it off the beach. Rockets were fired from the pier but the lines kept hitting the jagged stones and breaking. This was later said due to the lines being in a worn state. The lifeboat *Tyne* was manned but she had the same difficulty as the *Providence*. The *Tyne* went back to shore and picked up two of the coastguards with the intention of trying to approach the vessel again. Then a shout was

An engraving of the Port of Shields in the nineteenth century. Author's collection

raised from the spectators on land man overboard. One of the crew of the *Fowlis*, Peter McKenzie, was standing on the rocks. The *Tyne* went immediately to his rescue as it would only have taken one high wave to wash him from his precarious position. As the lifeboat approached McKenzie, Mr Hutchinson, a South Shields pilot, threw a lifebelt and the stranded sailor managed to grab it. A line was then thrown from the lifeboat and McKenzie secured it to his lifebelt and he was pulled to safety. The *Tyne* landed McKenzie amid cheers from the watching crowds. With the rocket apparatus on board the *Tyne* headed back to the *Fowlis*. Two lines were fired with the second landing on the deck and, by this means, Farquhar Fraser, the mate and George Fraser, the master, were rescued. The line then became entangled on the rocks and could not be used to save the three men remaining on the vessel. At this point the mainmast fell and the men could be seen standing in the weather gangway. A huge wave battered the ship and she began to break up. Her foremast fell and it was thought that the sailors were lost. Then one man, George Patience, was seen clinging to one piece of wreckage and the other two, Hugh Fraser and a boy, Alexander Jack, were seen clinging to another. Another heavy wave struck and engulfed the portion of wreckage that Fraser and the boy were clinging. The boy was gone but Fraser was then spotted drifting near to the pier. A salvage boat, *William Wake*, followed but did not get near in time to prevent Fraser being battered against the rocks. He was thrown up on the pier and died a few minutes later. Meanwhile, the third man, Patience, was still clinging to the wreckage. Wave after wave crashed against him but somehow he managed to hang on. As he drifted near to the pier, Robert Hardy, of North Shields, jumped into the water and

A view of South Shields in the nineteenth century. Author's collection

fastened a line around the exhausted man and he was pulled to safety. The body of the boy, Alexander Jack, was washed up later that day.

Around midday three lifeboats, *Providence, Tyne* and *Northumberland*, went to the aid of the coal-laden *Indus* of Newcastle with the *Northumberland* bringing off all her nine crew. She had struck the bar and drifted onto Herd Sand where she later broke up. About two hours later the schooner *Caesar* of Whitstable drifted off her course and came inside the Herd buoy, crossed the Herd and struck. Her crew were rescued by the *Northumberland* and the *Providence* lifeboats.

Other recorded losses around the Tyne during the Great Storm were a brigantine, *Constance Ellen*, with Captain Robinson and a crew of six wrecked at South Sand, South Shields, a snow, *Cambois*, with Captain Harrison and a crew of seven wrecked at Rockley Way, Whitburn, with the loss of four of the crew and a barque, *Christiane*, with Captain Stenersen and a crew of nine wrecked at the South Shields groyne.

A Goole billy boy, *Treaty*, was stranded on the Herd Sand. When the storm had abated, in order to float the vessel, twenty tons of her cargo of potatoes was thrown from her. Women, men and boys used anything that would float to get as near to the vessel as they safely could to collect the edible treasures as they were thrown overboard. The coal that strewed the shore, part of the cargo from the wrecked *Indus*, was another treasure there for the taking with no restrictions from the Customs men.

34. The *Stanley* and the *Friendship*, 1864

November 1864 brought a fierce storm to the North East coast and disaster to some of the ships that sought shelter in the Tyne. On the morning of Thursday 24 November a gale from the SE began to gather force and by early evening the wind was howling and the sea churning. All day ships had been running to the port for shelter.

The iron screw steamer, *Stanley*, was a ship of 200 feet in length and 552 tons burden that had been built by John Pile in Hartlepool for J Jack of Liverpool. She was launched in January 1859 and had been trading between London and Aberdeen. On this, her last, voyage she was carrying a cargo of livestock: pigs, cattle and sheep, and thirty passengers. The *Stanley* was near the Northumberland coast when the storm hit, so the master, Captain Howling, decided to head for the safety of the Tyne. The low-level lights at North Shields were not lit and, although it was only about 5pm, the darkness was almost impenetrable. The ship missed its entrance into the channel, instead striking the notorious Black Middens, rocks situated on the northern shore of the estuary near the Spanish Battery. The impact holed the ship and flooded her boiler fires. As if one terrible event was not enough, the spectators watched in horror as a Colchester schooner, *Friendship*, also trying to negotiate the channel, hit the rocks not far

An engraving from the Illustrated London News *of the* Stanley *when she was broken in two on the Black Middens in November 1864. Twenty-seven passengers and crew from the* Stanley *lost their lives along with six crew from the* Friendship, *which was wrecked at the same time.* Author's collection

from the *Stanley*. The Tynemouth lifeboat *Constance* was launched but when advised, mistakenly, that the crew of the ship were safe she was returned to shore. Word was brought that this information was wrong so the *Constance* was launched a second time. When she got near to the stranded vessel and the lifeboat crew were about to throw ropes aboard her, an enormous wave struck their boat, smashing oars and almost capsizing her. As the crew were trying to get the spare oars from the bottom of the boat another wave hit them and they were driven into the side of the *Friendship*. Four of the lifeboat crew jumped aboard the schooner. The crippled lifeboat, with a crew of six still aboard, was picked up by the *William Wake* and towed to safe landing at North Shields.

Meanwhile, the captain of the *Stanley*, seeing the dangerous situation they were in, ordered his crew to immediately throw the livestock overboard to try and lighten the vessel's load. News of the ship's plight quickly travelled and crowds of people gathered along the cliff top to wait for the outcome of the drama. From the distressed ship the cries of terrified women could be heard mingling with the sounds of lashing rain, wind and the thundering waves.

The *Providence* and *Tyne* lifeboats had been launched but could not get anywhere near the wreck site because of the high seas so all returned to their stations.

The Tynemouth Volunteer Life Brigade on exercise using a Breeches Buoy.
Author's collection

Lawrence Byrne, chief officer of the coastguard at Cullercoats, some Preventative men that were stationed at the Spanish Battery along with a number of boatmen and other residents of Tynemouth, readied the life saving apparatus and carried it down to the lower cliff. A rocket was fired to establish communication and when a whip line and hawser were connected to the vessel a breeches buoy was sent to begin bringing the passengers and crew ashore. A woman was helped into the cradle along with a seaman to accompany her but she was so terrified that she became hysterical and had to be taken back on board the ship. The other women were too frightened to make the attempt. One seaman, Andrew Campbell, and the second mate, James Kemp, were brought safely to shore by this method. On an attempt to bring a third man to safety in this manner the whip-line became entangled in the rocks and the cradle, with its passenger, was under water for a short time. Inch by inch those on shore managed to drag him a little closer but the line became entangled a second time. James Fry, George Bruce, Mr Ferguson and a fourth man waded into the boiling surf and managed to free the line so the cradle could be pulled to shore. Miraculously, its occupant was resuscitated and survived. Meanwhile the captain and officers of the *Stanley* had made the ship's lifeboat ready. Five women and four men climbed in but, as it was being lowered, the fore-davit broke, up-ending the small boat. Three of the occupants managed to scramble back aboard the ship but the others were swept away.

It was decided that the rocket apparatus was going to be of no use in its present position on the cliff so everything was loaded onto a cart and taken to the Low Lights to load onto a tug steamer. The hope was that a tug would be able to get near enough to the ship to attach a line and perform a rescue but none of the steam tug masters would run the risk of going out to sea in the severe weather conditions.

At about 10.30 pm a brig, *Ardwell*, crashed into the side of the *Stanley*. Some of the *Stanley's* crew managed to jump aboard the brig and were then picked up by the South Shields lifeboat.

At intervals loud crashing noises could be heard coming from the *Stanley* and at about 1am the steamer parted amidships and snapped in two. The fore part of the vessel was turned around by the heavy sea while the stern remained where it was. All that were on the stern were swept into the sea and drowned. At about 6 am on 25 November the Cullercoats rocket apparatus was used to cast lines from the shore to the fore part of the ship and nine passengers and about twenty crew men were rescued.

At about 11 pm the *Friendship* slid slowly from the rocks and, as she did so she was seen to turn over. The cries of the doomed could be heard for a few minutes until they and their vessel disappeared from sight.

Two of the lifeboat men that had jumped aboard the schooner, James Grant and Edmund Robson, were drowned but the other two, Joseph Bell and James Blackburn, were wearing cork lifebelts so managed to stay afloat and swim to shore.

Five seamen: Mr Falconer, James Gordon, James Wallis (a boy), John Sandland and Margaret Duncan (stewardess) and twenty-one passengers (about half of them women) from the *Stanley* lost their lives. Also drowned on that terrible night were the crew of six from the *Friendship*. In the days following the tragedy the carcasses of livestock along with human bodies and wreckage lined the shores.

The captain of the *Stanley*, Thomas Howling, had his master's certificate suspended until the formal inquiry was held in December of 1864. It was found that the loss had been caused by the violence of the sea, the absence of leading lights and other contributing factors. Howling was exonerated of all blame and his master's certificate was reinstated.

Amongst those that witnessed these events was an army officer, Captain John Morrison who, along with others, felt that more lives could have been saved by better organisation and training. He went to two of the most prominent residents of Tynemouth, John and Joseph Spence, with his ideas. This resulted in the establishment of the Volunteer Life Brigade whose members were trained in the workings of the rocket and other lifesaving apparatus so they could assist the coastguard in the event of shipwrecked crews that required rescue. The Tynemouth Volunteer Life Brigade was to be the first of many branches to be formed around Britain's coast and they have given service to those in peril on the sea from that day to the present.

A postcard dating from the early twentieth century depicting the Seaton Sluice Voluntary Life Brigade as they check their equipment. George Nairn

An engraving from the Illustrated London News *of the wreck of the SS* Earl Percy *in February 1865. She was struck by heavy seas when entering the Tyne and was driven onto the Black Middens where she was wrecked.* Author's collection

35. The *Earl Percy* and others, 1865

Once again the residents of Tynemouth were witness to the destruction of shipping on the seas within their locality. In February 1865 a 400 ton screw-steamer, *Earl Percy*, belonging to the Tyne Steam Shipping Company Limited, was sailing from Hamburg to the Tyne with Captain B Taylor, a crew of fifteen and one passenger, a merchant from Hamburg. She carried a cargo of sheep and cattle between decks. Although the wind was fairly moderate there was a heavy sea over Shields Bar and as the vessel passed over the Bar an immense wave caught her on her starboard quarter and drove her forward with extreme force onto the Black Middens. The *Stanley* had met her fate at this same spot the previous year and one of her boilers still remained on the rocks. Another wave then hit the *Earl Percy* and drove her further forward onto the rocks and the boiler. The sea continued to batter the vessel and she became holed in several places. The boiler was beneath her keel and, after a short time the vessel broke apart. Luckily for those aboard the tide was at an ebb so although the sea was still thundering against the vessel little more than spray showered her deck.

Those watching from shore wasted no time in launching a rescue. Lawrence Byrne, Chief Officer of the Cullercoats coastguard, ordered the rocket apparatus to be made ready on the beach opposite the

Soon to be a total loss, a vessel slowly flounders in the waters just off the coast of Tynemouth. Although a common occurrence during severe weather these disasters would see the shore lined with hundreds of spectators. Author's collection

stranded vessel. A line was fired and was made secure on the *Earl Percy* but this method of rescue was not required. The lifeboats came out in force not wanting a repeat of the previous year's tragedy of the *Stanley* and the *Friendship*. The *Providence* of South Shields under coxswain Joseph Smith, the Tyne under coxswain Andrew Harrison, the *Northumberland* under coxswain Gilbert Young, and the *California* under the coxswain of the *Constance*, James Gilbert, all headed towards their goal with speed. The *Providence* was the first to reach the ship and took every person off and landed them safely.

At low tide a party of men boarded the wrecked ship to save what they could of her cargo. The livestock was thrown overboard and hauled to shore by ropes, some landing more dead than alive. Tubs of lard and butter were saved and most of the crew's belongings. A number of local people were brought before the North Shields magistrates a few days later and fined for carrying off cargo that had washed ashore.

On the morning of 19 March of the same year a Hartlepool brig, *Border Chieftain*, was attempting to enter the Tyne in extremely heavy seas when a huge wave swamped her and, in the process, injured the wheel-man and damaged her steering gear. The lifeboat *Constance* was launched and rescued the pilot and crew of seven. The brig was later driven ashore at the Haven. That same afternoon the Colchester brigantine *Burton* struck at the end of the North Pier on the stones. The Tynemouth Volunteer Life Brigade fired a rocket line towards the ship but the crew did not manage to grasp hold of it. The *Constance* had been launched but before the lifeboat or another rocket line could reach the vessel she had begun to break up. Of the crew of six only the mate was found and brought to safety by the lifeboat crew. He had survived by managing to cling to a piece of wreckage.

<hr>

36. Volunteer Life Brigades, 1874

Another storm that left its mark on Tynemouth and Shields swept Britain towards the end of 1874. On the night of Saturday 28 November guns boomed from Tynemouth Castle and Her Majesty's gunboat *Castor*, giving alarms that a vessel was in distress. Members of the South Shields Voluntary Life Brigade were quickly assembled to await further instruction.

At 10.30 pm a vessel was seen driving onto the north side of the Herd Sand. A tug had attempted to tow the vessel off but failed when the tow-line broke. The lifeboats *Tyne* and *Tom Perry* had been launched and soon reached the ship where the *Tom Perry* safely took off Captain Martin and his crew of eight. The vessel was a Guernsey brig, *Lavinia*, which had sailed from London bound for the Tyne

A postcard depicting the premises of the Tynemouth Volunteer Life Brigade. The lifeboat house on the Black Middens can be seen to the bottom right. The house was built in 1865 and burned down in 1963. Author's collection

A sketch by Frank H Mason published in the Illustrated London News *of the wreck of the Norwegian barque* Diamant *at Tynemouth on 26 March 1898. As the barque entered the Tyne she was swamped by large waves which demolished her wheel house and jammed her steering. She drifted onto the Spanish Battery Rocks and struck stern first before swinging round broadside onto the rocks. The* Forester *lifeboat was launched but the* Diamant's *crew of eleven were rescued by the Tynemouth Volunteer Life Brigade using rocket lines from the shore. A short time later the barque went to pieces.* Author's collection

carrying a cargo of chalk. She was later found to have lost her rudder and had suffered only minor damage.

A watch was kept during the night and all remained quiet until a vessel trying to enter the river was driven forward and stranded on the south side of the South Pier. The Life Brigade fired a rocket line over the ship but it missed. A second line was fired and this time it was secured. One man, who had tried to grasp the line, fell but was caught by the captain and thus prevented from landing in the sea. All the crew were brought to land safely by means of the rocket line. This vessel was a Faversham schooner, *Scylla*, with a crew of five under the command of Captain George Carville.

The Tynemouth Voluntary Life Brigade had also been on watch throughout the night and following morning but it was to be afternoon before their services were required. A London schooner, *St Albans*, carrying a cargo of onions, was driven up and, with great force, struck the rubble at the north pier. The captain's wife and the mate were thrown into the foaming surf and drowned within yards of the land in sight of crowds of spectators powerless to help. One of the crew was thrown upon the deck and broke his thigh and the captain was also slightly injured. The Life Brigade quickly established a line of communication and Bryer, the seaman with the broken thigh, was brought off first followed by another seaman, Smeed, with the captain last.

Members of the Life Brigades, the coastguards and lifeboat crews were still on watch as the gale grew in intensity. During the early hours of Wednesday morning a large vessel was seen to be driven ashore near to the south pier. She was lying with her decks towards the sea and the huge waves were breaking over her. A rocket line was fired from the pier but it fell short being carried from its target by the wind. The second line hit its target but the crew failed to take hold of it. A loudspeaker was used but there was no response from the vessel. It was feared that either the crew were injured or had been washed overboard

A postcard of coxswain James Gilbert (wearing a cork lifejacket) who was awarded the RNLI Silver Medal in 1886 for his long and valuable service in the lifeboat. Author's collection

before the ship grounded. A third and a fourth line was fired but there was still no response. The ship broke up very quickly and there was little left to see where she had been. During a search for bodies a bible was picked up with an inscription showing that the vessel had been the *Henry Cooke* of South Shields. The master, John Swallow Waddle, and his crew of seventeen had all perished. The captain of another vessel that made it safely to the Tyne said that he had seen the *Henry Cooke* on Tuesday afternoon in a disabled state. He had not sees any crew on deck and had assumed that they had already been swept overboard.

Not long after the first tragedy another vessel, a schooner, drove onto the Herd Sand. Three of the Life Brigade members, Benjamin Heron, William Groat and Thomas Wood went across the sand to communicate with those on board the schooner. Those on board felt they were safe and did not want to leave their vessel. As the three men had been talking the tide had come in and they became virtually cut off from land. They began to wade through the water which was almost waist high. Heron reached safety but Groat and Wood were still struggling to reach shore. The two men climbed up a bathing post but then became worried that it would not hold their weight so stepped down into the sea again. They managed to get hold of a large piece of timber from the wreckage of the *Henry Cooke*, and on this they were able to paddle to shore. The crew of the schooner waded to shore at low tide at daylight on Wednesday morning.

⚓

37. Storm Times Two, 1876

During the first weekend of December 1876 a violent SE gale swept the north-east coast. The Shields and Tynemouth Volunteer Life Brigades and the lifeboat crews were on watch all through Saturday night and Sunday.

The first casualty to be reported was that of a Cullercoats fishing coble. The small boat was caught in the storm on Saturday afternoon just offshore from Tynemouth. The Cullercoats lifeboat *Palmerston* was launched but by the time she reached the scene the coble had capsized drowning Selby Nixon, George Armstrong and George Nicholson. A boy, Thomas Stoker, was floating on one of the oars and was the only one to be rescued.

The next casualty was reported on Sunday morning when a quantity of wreckage washed up on the shore at North Shields. Amongst the items was a ship's small boat on which was printed *Prince* of Glasgow. Upon enquiries being made it was found that the *Prince* was a screw-steamer which had sailed, fully loaded with cast and pig iron, from Middlesbrough bound for Grangemouth. She had sunk between the

A postcard depicting the River Tyne and Tynemouth Piers in the early twentieth century. Author's collection

north and south pier buoys at the entrance to Shields Harbour taking her crew of fourteen with her. Captain Francis Donaldson, George Woodrow, the mate, and crew Alexander Mather, Henry Buckhannon, William McLaren, William Pitblado, Henry Johnson, John Hegeson, Henry Stupple, James Day, Archibald Hamilton, John Querie, Joseph Ellis and Robert Donkinson had all drowned. There was only one survivor and that was the ship's dog which managed to swim ashore. A subsequent inquiry found that she had foundered because of improper stowage of her cargo in the forehold which caused her to be top heavy

On Sunday night a Whitstable brigantine, *Seven Sons*, on trying to

A postcard depicting Albert Edward Dock, North Shields in the late nineteenth century. Author's collection

enter the harbour was driven onto the Black Middens. The alarm guns were fired and the lifeboat quickly launched but because the tide was low no assistance could be given. The Life Brigade launched rocket lines and by this means Captain Kemp, his son and five men were rescued before the vessel became a total wreck.

On Tuesday 19 December the second storm of that month hit the coast with winds blowing ENE which increased in violence to gale-force 9 over the following two days. Yorkshire, Northumberland and Durham all saw destruction to shipping and loss of life but Tynemouth suffered perhaps more than elsewhere. Early on Thursday morning a Newcastle steamer, *Claremont*, was the first to require assistance as she was driven behind the south pier. The Life Brigade was able to rescue the crew of nineteen and the wife and child of one of the engineers. The next vessel's crew were not to be so lucky. At about 7 am a North Shields iron screw-steamer, *Tyne*, was driven onto the end of the south pier and was almost immediately dashed to pieces. The Life Brigade fired their rockets but to no avail, Captain A Lawlan and all sixteen of his crew were lost. A London steamship, *Fenella*, was the next to come ashore at the pier. Her crew managed to walk off at low tide.

At about 11am a Blyth snow, *First of May*, sailing from the Thames to her home port was driven onto the Herd Sand and wrecked. Again the Life Brigade was able to give assistance and Captain R Coulson and his crew of seven were rescued.

A Whitstable schooner, *Albion*, was caught in mid-channel and driven onto the Bar. Four rockets were fired by the Life Brigade and Captain E Paris and his crew of five were taken off by rocket lines and the lifeboat, *Charles Dibden*. A Hartlepool screw-steamer, *Blenheim*, could not enter her home port because of the heavy tide, so had made for the Tyne instead. At the same time the rescue of the *Albion's* crew was being carried out the *Blenheim* was crossing the Bar. A huge wave struck her broadside driving her against the end of the south pier

A postcard depicting Cullercoats Bay, c1904. Author's collection

where she broke in two. Captain Bertram (or Bethune) and eighteen of his crew of nineteen got off safely. Some managed to leap from the vessel to the pier and the others were taken off by the Life Brigade. Of those that jumped to the pier, a few were injured, with one sustaining a broken leg. The cook, Nathaniel Richardson of West Hartlepool, was killed when he was crushed between the vessel and the pier as he jumped.

A Barnstaple schooner, *New Cornwall*, which had been sailing from Brussels to Newcastle fully loaded with a cargo of marble and ore, foundered near the south pier with the loss of all the crew of five. The *John Liddle* of Newcastle, sailing from London to Sunderland, struck the south pier and was driven ashore at the north sands. The crew managed to save themselves in their own boat.

<hr />

38. A Heavy Toll, 1880

On Wednesday 27 October the piers at Tynemouth were almost obliterated by the driving rain and the mountainous seas. The Shields and Tynemouth Volunteer Life Brigades were on duty all through the night. At about 8 am the guns were fired to announce that there was a vessel in distress. A Danish schooner, *Johanna*, sailing from Rochester for Middlesbrough had got foul of the south pier. The collision had carried away her bowsprit and holed her. She drifted helplessly on to the end of the South Shields fish pier and, within minutes, began to go to pieces. The lifeboat *Northumberland* was quickly at the wreck but it was to be too late. Only the mate was still aboard, Captain J Plough and two seamen had been washed overboard and drowned long before the vessel had reached the Tyne.

Shortly afterwards a North Shields steam-trawler, *Wonga*, was seen trying to make harbour. A huge sea obliterated her for a few seconds and when she reappeared she was bottom up, Captain Patton and his crew of five were gone. About an hour later a North Shields iron trawler, *Flying Huntsman*, suffered the same fate with the loss of Captain A Bartram and his crew of six.

Later on the afternoon of the same day a Yarmouth schooner, *Isis*, with her sails in tatters, narrowly missed being capsized. She drove ashore on the Herd Sand where Captain T Anderson and his crew of five were rescued by the Life Brigade.

The *Astley* of West Hartlepool drove ashore north of Cullercoats. Captain Bryson and her crew of five were rescued by the Cullercoats Life Brigade. John Bryson, the captain s son, would not leave the ship's pets, a poodle and a cat. As Bryson had left the ship with the animals in his arms, the cat had jumped back aboard. Bryson had gone after it

Looking down onto the lifeboat house at Cullercoats Bay c1910. Author's collection

and eventually climbed into the lifeboat holding the two pets. Some of the remains of this ship can still be seen at low tide.

At 8pm a Faversham brigantine, *Harry Clem*, sailing from Whitstable to Seaham, came ashore south of the pier and keeled over. Captain William Willard and a seaman were washed overboard and drowned. The four remaining crew were rescued by the Life Brigade.

Other vessels were stranded, wrecked and foundered, some because of breaking free from their moorings. Although there was considerable loss of life there were also many seamen who gave thanks that they had narrowly escaped a watery grave.

39. A Busy Watch, 1882

Early on the morning of Monday 4 December 1882 a severe easterly gale suddenly sprang up and continued unabated for a week. There was hardly a port anywhere around the coast that was unaffected. Abnormally high tides kept the piers at Tynemouth awash and the entrance to the Tyne had the appearance of a boiling cauldron.

At about 1.30 pm a Hamburg barque, *Rheinland*, was in tow of the steam-tug Skylark heading towards the entrance to the Tyne when the tow-line parted. The barque was driven onto the rocks at the Spanish Battery. The lifeboats *Forester* and *Tom Perry* were launched. With enormous difficulty they managed to reach the barque with the *Forester* taking off two of the crew and the *Tom Perry* the remaining twelve.

By nightfall snow and sleet was falling making visibility poor. The Life Brigades and lifeboat men were out in force keeping watch in case their services were required. A few vessels managed to enter the harbour safely but, at about 10.30 pm lights were seen to be burning from a vessel in the bay at the back of the north pier. About an hour later the lookout announced the approach of a vessel which seemed to be struggling to make headway. She neared the piers and, on entering the broken water, drifted towards the south pier and then disappeared from sight. Watchers immediately went to where the vessel had last been observed but there was no sign of her anywhere. They continued their vigil but it was assumed that perhaps she had been a small vessel and had made harbour without being seen due to the poor visibility. At about 2 am, at low tide, men went to the Haven to see if any wreckage had washed ashore. To their dismay they found the sand strewn with bottles of oil, casks and other items of cargo. There was also a name board which identified the vessel as the schooner *Catherine and Mary* which had been bound from London for the Tyne. She had foundered with the loss of Captain J Turner and his crew of four.

A Norwegian brig, *Olaf Kyrre,* had been loaded and left the Tyne on Sunday bound for her home port. When the storm broke Captain Anderson struggled to keep on his course. On Tuesday morning a huge sea washed over the vessel's deck carrying away the ship's two small boats, the bulwarks and the side lights. The cargo shifted and the brig sprung a leak. The vessel was virtually unmanageable but they ran

Cobles and the lifeboat house on the beach at Cullercoats in the early twentieth century. Author's collection

before the gale and made Souter Light. At about 7 pm they flashed lights for a pilot to try to get them into harbour but a sudden squall drove the brig towards the south pier. Captain Anderson decided to try to run for the beach but the hold was carrying a few feet of water and the crew were exhausted with working the pumps all day so all control was lost. The vessel was driven onto the huge stones that had been placed around the unfinished south pier to protect the structure.

The crew took to the main rigging but as they did so the brig turned with her bow facing out to sea. The captain ordered the crew to move to the fore rigging because he did not think that the mainmast would hold for long. For almost three hours the crew remained in their dangerous position being constantly drenched with huge waves. Two rocket lines went over the rigging but the crew could not get to them and a third line broke. Meanwhile the South Shields lifeboat men had manned and launched the lifeboat *Tyne*. With the huge seas washing over them, and in very real danger of capsizing, the lifeboat pulled slowly towards the stricken brig and succeeded in taking off all her exhausted but extremely grateful crew.

The crew that manned the lifeboat consisted of Andrew James and Martin Purvis, Robert Chambers, Richard and Ralph Harrison, Thomas Heslop, John Cairns, John Blair, R Flett, Robinson Bell, John Whale and Anthony Hogg.

⁕

40. More Casualties, 1901

Shields, Tynemouth and Cullercoats had their share of shipping disasters along with the rest of the north-east coast during the gales of Tuesday 12 and Wednesday 13 November 1901. The first vessel was an Inverness smack, *Golden Lilly*, which had sailed from Yarmouth. Her crew endeavoured to keep the vessel out at sea but they could not hold her and she was driven ashore at Shields. The men floated bladders attached to lines which they tied around their waists and by this means rescuers were able to pull the master, Alexander Smith, the owner, Mr Baker and the crew of six safely to shore. The second vessel to come to grief was a Norwegian barque, *Christina* (or *Christiane*), carrying a cargo of ice from Langesund to the Tyne. Captain T S Stenersen and his crew of eight had seen the Souter light before realising they were in danger. Their vessel was driven onto the pier and keeled over onto her side. The crew crawled along the jibboom and managed to reach the pier. Following these two ships was a Littlehampton barque, *Constance Ellen*, which had been sailing from her home port to Borrowstones with a cargo of iron railway tracks. When off Whitby several of her sails had been carried away by the gale so her captain, A Robinson, decided

A postcard depicting Polly Donkin, a fishwife from Cullercoats. Three Cullercoats women were awarded an RNLI Gold Badge for their tireless efforts of fundraising for the cause. Polly was eighty-two when her award was presented in 1939 by the Duke of Kent. Author's collection

A postcard depicting the breakwaters at Cullercoats c1910. Author's collection

to run for Shields. Despite the efforts of himself and his crew of six, the ship was driven onto the Herd Sand. After several hours of being stranded in this perilous position all the men were eventually got off before the vessel became a total wreck.

On the second day of the storm a Norwegian iron barque, *Inga*, was driven into an outcrop of rocks offshore from Cullercoats. She hit the rocks with such force that she capsized and only one of her crew of sixteen survived.

41. Gallantry Medals

1827: Silver Medal to Alexander Donkin of Cullercoats who rescued the master of the sloop *James* from the sea after an initial attempt at rescue by nine local men failed because of the heavy seas.

1829: Silver Medal to Henry Strachan, pilot, for the rescue of five from a Customs House boat on 1 December 1828. Strachan and his son had saved the five people from certain death by going to their assistance in a boat of only fourteen feet (approx. 4m.) in length.

1832: Silver Medal to William Tully, pilot, for the rescue of the master and two seamen from the sloop *Friendship* wrecked off the Spanish Battery near Shields Harbour on 16 September 1830. Tully and three other men had tried to assist in a coble but the sea was too high. Tully swam from rock to rock until he was near enough to throw a rope to the vessel.

1839: Silver Medal to Thomas Thorpe, storekeeper of the rockets, for the rescue of eleven by means of Dennett's Rockets from the *Progress,* stranded on 12 March 1839.

1843: Silver Medal to John Cunningham for the rescue by rocket apparatus of an apprentice from the *Constantia*, wrecked at Tynemouth on 23 January 1843.

1851: Silver Medal to William Wheeler, a pilot. He was piloting the Danish brig *Margaretta* up the Tyne when he saw two of her crew go overboard. Wheeler dived into the water and managed to save one of the men. He had also been involved in the rescue of four of the crew of the Sunderland brig *Percy* when she was wrecked on the rocks at Tynemouth three years previously.

1853: Silver Medal to coxswain John Redford of Cullercoats for rescuing a young boy from a wrecked fishing boat in which another two people drowned.

1864: Silver Medal to Lawrence Byrne, a coastguard, for his bravery and perseverance in the rescue by rocket apparatus of thirty-eight people from the steamer *Stanley* and the schooner *Friendship* when they were wrecked at Tynemouth on 24 November 1864.

1886: Silver Medal to coxswain James Gilbert for his long and valuable service to the lifeboat.

1898: Silver Second Service Clasp to James Gibson on his retirement as coxswain.

1898: Silver Medal to coxswain Andrew Taylor of Cullercoats on his retirement.

1913: Silver Medals to Captain HE Burton, coxswain, Robert Smith, (and coxswain, Anthony Nixon, of the *Cambois* lifeboat) for their assistance in rescuing the crew of the *Dunhelm* wrecked off Blyth on 11 January 1913. Gold Medals and watches were presented to each member of the *Tyne* lifeboat crew on behalf of the public in the locality.

1915: Gold Medal to Captain HE Burton and coxswain Robert Smith and Silver Medals to second coxswain James Brownlee and Lieutenant Basil Hall, lifeboat inspector, for the rescue of the last fifty survivors from the hospital ship *Rohilla* which ran aground on a reef at Saltwick Nab, south of Whitby, on 31 October to 1 November 1914. The Tynemouth Trust also awarded special Gold Medals to all twelve men of the crew of the Tynemouth lifeboat *Henry Vernon*.

1916: Empire Gallantry Medal (in 1940 to become the George Cross) to Major Burton for his splendid services on taking charge of the lifeboat *Henry Vernon* in its services to the *Rohilla*. Silver Second Service Clasps to Coxswain Robert Smith and Second Coxswain James Brownlee for the rescue of sixteen from the steamship *Muristan* which stranded on 19 November 1916.

1918: Silver Cup to each member of the lifeboat crew by His Majesty King of Norway for their rescue of 118 crew and passengers from the Norwegian steamship *Bessheim* on 19 November 1916. Medals were also awarded to the crew of the lifeboat *Tom Perry*.

1926: Bronze Medal to Ordinary Seaman Michael Campbell RNVR for his gallant conduct in plunging into the river and rescuing a man who was thrown into the water when his boat capsized near the coble landing on 8 August 1926.

1931: A Gold Badge to Polly Donkin, a seventy-three-year-old fishwife of Cullercoats, in recognition of her dedicated service in collecting funds on behalf of the RNLI.

1939: A Gold Badge to Mrs Tom Lisle, a fishwife of Cullercoats, in recognition of her dedicated service in collecting funds on behalf of the RNLI.

1941: Bronze Medals to Edward Selby Davidson, Honorary Secretary of the Tynemouth RNLI Branch, and coxswain George Lisle for their gallant conduct in the rescue of twenty-two from the Norwegian motor vessel *Oslo Fiord* which went ashore south of the Tyne on 8 December 1940.

1942: A Gold Badge to Bella Mattison for her dedicated service in collecting funds on behalf of the RNLI.

1959: Morley Medal of the Outward Bound Trust to Kenneth Smith, a member of the lifeboat crew.

1959: Royal Humane Society's Testimonial on Parchment to Robert Rutherford, a member of the lifeboat crew, for the part he played in rescuing an elderly man from the freezing waters of the Tyne at North Shields in January.

1974: Bronze Medals to crew members Trevor Fryer and Frederick Arkley in recognition of the courage and determination they displayed when the inshore lifeboat rescued the crew of three and a boy from the tug *Northsider* which had been driven onto the Black Middens on 10 March 1974.

1982: Thanks of the Institution inscribed on vellum to helmsman Trevor Fryer in recognition of his determination and seamanship when nine people were rescued by the D-Class inflatable lifeboat from the motor boat *Blue Fin* on 11 April.

1986: Silver Medal to coxswain John Hogg in recognition of the courage, determination and seamanship he displayed when the lifeboat rescued the crew of three from the fishing vessel *La Morlaye* on 15 April 1986.

1998: A Letter of Thanks signed by the Chairman to coxswain Martin Kenny and also a Letter of Thanks signed by the Chairman to crew members Edwin Chapple, Geoffrey Cowan, Kevin Mole and Michael Nugent for their services to the yacht, *Signature,* on 3 April.

Conclusion

*A*s the nineteenth century was delegated to the past, with it went the wooden-masted sailing ships. Vessels of stronger construction and new, safer, technology took over meaning there were far fewer shipwrecks and much less loss of life. Sadly, this was to change during the First and Second World Wars. The twentieth century once again saw wrecks littering the coastline and families losing their loved ones to the sea. Now much of the wreckage lying on the beaches, rocks and sea-bed are not wood but metal and the cause often not the weather, but man.

During the years of the two world wars the North East coast was a prime target for the enemy who caused many casualties by the use of aircraft fire, submarines and mines. Hartlepool and West Hartlepool were particularly vulnerable because they were extremely industrial. The first soldier in the First World War and the first Civil Defence worker to be killed in the Second World War were both from Hartlepool.

Lifeboat crews and fishermen, although on a reserve list, were usually exempt from being called up because of the nature of their work. Targeting fishing vessels was important to the enemy as destroying sources of food assisted their cause. If the enemy targeted a fishing vessel, the crews, not being military, were usually allowed to leave before the vessel was sunk. The following accounts are only a minute portion of the terrible toll those years inflicted upon shipping on the north-east coast.

First World War
On 27 August 1914, offshore from Sunderland, a Danish schooner *Gaea* carrying a cargo of coke from Sunderland to her home port of Svendborg struck a mine and sunk. The mine was thought to have been laid by a German submarine. In the same year some of the fishing vessels that were lost through striking mines around the vicinity of the Tyne were *Crathie, Barley Rig* and *Rosella.*

Offshore from Hartlepool in 1916, after the crews abandoning ship, the fishing vessels *Girl's Friend, Ben Aden* and *Seal* were sunk by German submarines. In December of the same year, a Newcastle steamship *Burnhope* struck a submerged object which caused an explosion. A second explosion followed seconds later which caused major damage to the vessel. The crew abandoned ship and were picked up by a vessel in the vicinity but shortly after being rescued Captain J Rodger suffered a heart attack and died.

After the end of hostilities HM Submarine G-11 was on her first peacetime patrol and had sailed from the River Tees. On 22 November 1918, as she was heading for the Coquet Island lighthouse, she encountered dense fog and struck the shoreline near Howick. Her bow ploughed high onto the shelving rocks with the damage allowing water to flood in to her engine room causing her to keel over. Captain George Bradshaw ordered one of his men, Lieutenant Smith, to swim to shore with a line. The line was secured and all but two of her crew reached safety by this means. George Nairn

On 29 April 1916 a British steamship, *Teal*, carrying a general cargo from Leith to London was torpedoed and sunk offshore from Seaham by the German submarine *UB-27*. The survivors from the *Teal* reached Hartlepool in their own ship's boats. Also offshore from Seaham a Grimsby fishing trawler, *King James*, was captured by a German submarine. The crew abandoned ship after which the trawler was sunk by its captors. In August both a Rotterdam steamship, *Zeeland*, and a Grimsby fishing trawler, *Helvetia*, were captured offshore from Sunderland by German submarines. After the crews abandoned ship both vessels were sunk by the enemy. Near Tynemouth, after the crews being forced to abandon ship, the Germans sunk the fishing vessels *Blessing, Annie Henderson, Peep O Day, Newark Castle, Watchful* and *Bute*.

On 31 January 1917 a Middlesbrough tug, *Ida Duncan*, struck a mine just off the South Gare lighthouse near Teesmouth. Captain I J Baker and her crew of five all perished. On 6 February a Grangemouth steamship, *Vestra*, was torpedoed and sunk near Hartlepool with the loss of two lives. In the same month the fishing trawlers *Euston* and

Recepto were sunk after striking mines. Another casualty was a London steamship, *John Miles*, which sank after an explosion with the loss of ten of the crew of fourteen, one dying aboard the rescue vessel.

The *Hero*, a tug owned by the Tees Tug Co, was leaving Sunderland on 28 March 1917 when she struck a mine at the entrance to the River Wear. Another tug that was in the vicinity took three survivors off the sinking vessel but the master could not be found. A London steamship, *Firelight*, was torpedoed by a German submarine close to the Tynemouth piers. The survivors were picked up in their ship's boat by a steamship in the vicinity. Another London steamship, *Rio Colorado*, was also torpedoed and sunk near the North Pier with the loss of her captain and crew of nine.

On 12 May 1918, offshore between Sunderland and Seaham, a West Hartlepool steamship, *Haslingdean*, was torpedoed and sunk by the German submarine *UB-21*. Survivors were picked up by a patrol vessel but the master and three of his crew lost their lives. On 13 August a Swedish steamship, *Jonkoping I*, carrying a cargo of iron from Gothenburg to Hull was torpedoed and sunk offshore from Tynemouth by the German submarine *UB-112*.

Second World War
In November 1939 a Liverpool steamship, *Carmarthen Coast*, struck a German mine offshore from Sunderland with two men killed in the explosion. A month later a Bruges steamship, *Rosa*, was lost in the same manner near Tynemouth Breakwater. On 14 December of the same year a tanker, *Inverlane*, which had been requisitioned by the Admiralty to be sunk as a block ship to help close the Scapa Flow

Two destroyers ashore, probably at Tynemouth. In this image military and civilian personnel appear to be salvaging the cargo. M Sherris

A closer view of the same two destroyers as in the previous image. The pennant identifies one as the H78 Class F which was built by Vickers and Armstrong of Barrow in Furness. After this mishap she was successfully re-floated and was sold in 1949 to the Dominican Navy and renamed Generalisimo. M Sherris

The Cairnglen *in October 1940 as she was being wrecked near the rocks at Camel Island, Marsden.* M Sherris

The Norwegian five-deck passenger liner, the Oslofjord, *was sailing from Liverpool to Newcastle in ballast after being refitted as a troopship. As she neared Tynemouth on 1 January 1940 she struck a German mine and was subsequently wrecked.* M Sherris

approach from the west was on her way to her destination. She struck and detonated a German mine. Three of the crew were killed and many more were injured in the blast. The survivors abandoned ship and the vessel drifted, still burning, for a few days until she beached near Whitburn. Part of her was salvaged and eventually towed to Scapa Flow and sunk. It was ironic that the *Inverlane* had originally been built in the 1930s for Germany.

On 22 October 1940 a Newcastle steamship, *Cairnglen*, was nearing the end of a long voyage from Montreal via Leith to the Tyne. She was carrying a general cargo including wheat, bacon and engines. It was early morning and foggy when her captain saw what he thought was the buoy for the entrance to the Tyne. He instructed what he thought to be the proper course to be set but the buoy was actually marking the southern limit of the channel. The steamer was almost a mile too far south of her correct destination and she ran straight onto the rocks of a reef close to Camel Island at Marsden.

At 11.48pm on 20 June 1941 as the SS Ilse was entering the Port of Hartlepool she struck a mine which broke her back. Most of the crew were aft at the time and managed to get into the ship's boat and were towed to safety by a Pilot Cutter. One man was killed and three injured in the explosion. Much of the vessel was later salvaged. Griffith Hatton

This photo from the 1940s shows the workings of the salvage of a vessel. The tube shaped object to the right of the image is a camel and these were used in the raising or salvage of a ship. They would be flooded and then emptied using compressed air similar to flotation air bags that are in use today. By this means the ship would be lightened. M Sherris

The 223 ton trawler, Eileen Duncan, *sunk by enemy aircraft at North Shields on 30 September 1941.* M Sherris

The *Cairnglen* was heavily damaged and as the tide rose the seas became heavy. At this time she was too far from shore for Rocket lines to reach her but then she began to drift further inshore. She struck rocks again and, pounded by the waves, her back broke. About twenty of her crew lowered a ship's boat and somehow made it to shore through the heavy surf. The ship was now within reach of the rocket apparatus and a line was fired. The remaining crew were terrified and it was not until a member of the Life Brigade, William Burton, went across to the ship in a bosun's chair that they could be persuaded to leave by this means.

Although the *Cairnglen* was not targeted by the enemy she was still a casualty of the war. Tugs and other vessels that could have assisted to re-float her were all engaged elsewhere in trying to prevent or assist casualties of mines and enemy fire.

In April of 1840 the Norwegian *Oslofjord* had been involved in a

The Greek cargo ship, Eugenia Chandris, *in 1943 as she was sinking after colliding with the wreck of the* Oslofjord. M Sherris

collision and had been laid up at New York. Later that year it was decided to re-fit her to do service as a troopship. Carrying a general cargo as well as nearly 14,000 bags of mail she arrived at Gourock Bay on 28 November where her troops disembarked and her cargo was to be discharged. The following day the troops were called back aboard as she had been ordered by the Admiralty to go to Newcastle-upon-Tyne escorted by a destroyer *Vimy*. On 1 December, when near to the entrance to the Tyne, she struck a German mine. Captain Ole Bornemann Bull and four of his crew were on the bridge where three were knocked down by the explosion. The helmsman, Yngvar Halvorsen, and the captain were injured and unconscious. The captain regained consciousness soon after but was badly injured. Several tugs and a pilot came to her aid but she was refused entrance to port because her engine rooms were flooding rapidly and if she sunk would block the entrance to the Tyne. There was no option other than to beach her near the Tynemouth South Pier.

The helmsman died of his injuries the same day and the captain was taken to hospital with a crushed vertebrae. Some of those aboard were taken off by the Cullercoats lifeboat, *Westmoreland*, and some by the Tynemouth Lifeboat, *John Pyemont*. A few remained on board until 8 December. During this time well over half the bags of mail were taken to safety by volunteers. The weather became severe and the ship began to break up so the last of those aboard were taken off by the *John Pyemont*. Towards the end of January, during severe weather, the

Oslofjord broke in two, capsized and sunk.

Three years later, on 15 March 1943, a Greek cargo ship, *Eugenia Chandris*, struck the seaward end of the wreck of the *Oslofjord* and sunk. Both wrecks lie close together and are regularly visited by divers.

On the same day, prior to the *Oslofjord* striking a mine, a similar fate had befallen a tanker, *British Officer*, as she entered the Tyne. When she was between the piers her engine detonated a vibratory mine which caused her aft section to flood and kill forty-seven of her crew. She sank with her bow still afloat which blocked the Tyne so the fore section had to be towed into port. The stern section was disbursed by explosives and divers.

A Portsmouth paddle steamer, *Southsea*, had been hired by the Admiralty and converted to do service as a minesweeper. On 16 February 1941 she was carrying out her delegated duty between the Tynemouth Piers when, ironically, she detonated a German mine and sunk. Seven of her crew were killed. Later that year she was moved ashore but was eventually declared a total wreck and sold for scrap.

Many of these wrecks still lie on the sea-bed, home to hundreds of species of marine life, and visited by divers when weather and visibility permits. Some are just lumps of twisted metal and others are virtually complete. The ocean-going vessels that became casualties of the war and now lie in silence in their watery graves all have one thing in common: as testimonials to man's inhumanity to man.

ources

Tees Archaeology Archives
Hartlepool Arts and Museums Archives
Returns of Wreck for Hartlepool and Seaton Carew, 1860-1907
London Illustrated News, 3 December 1864
Extract from the *Ladies Auxiliary Magazine*, c1896
Durham Chronicle, 1815
South Durham Herald and Stockton Journal
Stockton and Hartlepool Mercury
Northern Daily Mail
Newcastle Courant
Newcastle Weekly Courant
Newcastle Daily Chronicle
The History of the Tees Pilots, D S Hellier, 1982
The Illustrated Dictionary of North East Shipwrecks, Peter Collings
The History of the Seaham Lifeboats, Jeff Morris, 1988
The History of the Cullercoats Lifeboats, Jeff Morris, 1994
The History of the Tynemouth Lifeboats, Jeff Morris, 1995
Shipwreck Index of the British Isles, The East Coast, Volume III,
Richard and Bridget Larn, 1997

Glossary

Ballast: weight put in a vessel s hold or seawater pumped into the tanks to increase her stability.

Barque or Bark: sailing vessel with at least three masts, fore & aft rigged mizzen mast.

Barquentine: sailing vessel with three or more masts with a square rigged foremast and only fore and aft rigged sails on the main, mizzen and other masts.

Bow: front or forward end of a vessel.

Bowsprit: a pole extending from the prow providing an anchor point for the forestays.

Brig: sailing vessel with two masts of which at least one is square rigged.

Brigantine: a smaller version of a Brig.

Davit: a crane device for raising and lowering, anchors, small boats and cargo.

Fore-mast: the first mast.

Full rigged: square rigged with three or more masts.

Galleon: sailing vessel that is multi-decked with three to five masts.

Hold: the interior where cargo is stored.

Jibboom: the spar extending forward from, and secured on top of the bowsprit.

Keel: the principal structure running lengthwise along the centreline from bow to stern to which the frames are attached.

Ketch: sailing vessel with two masts, the mizzen mast forward of the rudder post.

Main-mast: the tallest mast usually located towards the centre of the vessel.

Mizzen-mast: the third mast, typically shorter than the fore-mast.

Prow: the fore or front of the vessel.

Schooner: sailing vessel fore and aft, two or more masts, after masts as tall as the main mast.

Sloop: sailing vessel that has a fore and aft rig and carries a single mast.

Snow: sailing vessel with two masts and trysail mast.

Staysail: sails that are carried between masts.

Stern: the rear of the vessel.

Square rigged: the most common type of rigging in which the sails are on one or more masts set from yards, wooden spars attached to the masts, and are square in shape. These are fore and aft sails along the keel parallel to the length of the vessel.

Try-sail: a small fore and aft sail hoisted in a storm to keep the vessel's bow to the wind.

Windlass: a hand operated winch used primarily for raising the anchor and also for raising and lowering the mainmast.

Index

People

Adamson, John 107
Altensal, Captain 91
Anderson, Albert 19, 50
Anderson, Captain 123, 125
Anderson, James 19
Arkley, Frederick 130
Armstrong, Captain 75
Armstrong, George 120
Atkinson, W 45
Aucoin, Francois 39
Backhouse, Thomas 17
Bailey, Frederick 90
Bailey, John 26
Baker, Mr, 126
Baldwin, Captain 79
Barlow, Miss Sarah 16
Barnet, Henry Graham 61
Bartram, Captain A 123
Belk, Alfred 49
Bell, Joseph 114
Bell, Robinson 126
Beeching, James 98
Bennison, Lieutenant WH 70
Bertram, Captain 123
Bevan, Herman 52
Blackburn, James 114
Blacklin 89
Blackin, Richard J 86
Blair, John 126
Blake, Percy 90
Blanch, William 30
Blenkinsopp, Thomas 44–45
Boagey, Francis 21
Boagey, John 21
Bolton, Thomas 76-7
Bond, Robert 107
Bowes, Rigger 49
Bowman, John 27
Boyle, AG 49
Bradshaw, Captain
George 132
Broderick, John 31
Brown, 91
Brown, Captain Burton 41
Brownlee, James 129
Bruce, George 113
Bruce, John 88
Brunswick, Captain 25
Bryer 118
Bryson, Captain 123-4
Bryson, John 123
Buckhannon, Henry 121
Buckley, D 45
Bull, Captain Ole
Bornemann 138
Bulmer, Harry 19
Bulmer, John 19
Burdon, John 89
Burnham, J 45
Burton, Major HE 97, 129
Burton, Richard 44–45

Burton, William 137
Byrne, Lawrence 113, 116,
129
Cairns, John, 126
Calmer, Captain 41
Calvert, Paul 30
Cambridge, J 21, 49, 58
Campbell, Alexander 76
Campbell, Charles 52, 57
Campbell, James 26
Campbell, Michael 130
Carville, Captain George
118
Cedergren, Carl 61
Chambers, Robert 126
Chapple, Edwin 130
Ching, Mr 84
Chisholm, Captain 34
Chilholm, John 105
Cimmermann, Captain 42
Clarke, George 26
Cole, Captain 77
Cole, Thomas 35
Cole, William 22, 35
Colley, Adam 88
Cook, James 90
Cooke, Thomas 19
Cooper, Boyes 34
Corner, R 49, 58
Coulson, Captain R 122
Coulson, James 21
Coulson, Thomas 21
Cowan, Geoffrey 130
Cowell, George 36-37
Cowell, Hannah 37
Cox, Alexander 103
Crooke, Captain 84
Crosby, Alison 34
Cross, Harry 59
Crowder, Captain 22
Cunningham, John 129
Cuthbertson, John 19, 50
Davis, Captain 99
Davis, George 26
Davidson, Edward Selby
130
Davison, EF 58
Davison, George 58, 87
Davison, John 21
Davison, W 77, 92
Dawson, Thomas 67
Day, Captain C 25
Day, James 121
Delepine, Captain 90
Denton, JHR 49
Dibdin, Charles 97
Dodds, William 105
Donaldson, Captain
Francis 121
Donkin, Alexander 128
Donkin, Polly 127, 130
Donkinson, Robert 121

Douglas, William 22
Duncan, Margaret 114
Dyson, Captain 84
Eldon, Lord 37
Elliott, J 50
Ellis, Joseph 121
Evans, Captain William 21
Falconer, Mr 144
Fenwick GJ 96
Ferguson, Mr 113
Filburn, John 53
Flett, R 126
Fox, Captain 100
Francis, Robert 105
Francole, Lienel 90
Franklin, John 19, 42, 50,
54, 57, 67-8
Franklin, Matthew 42, 45,
67
Franklin, William 19, 50
Fraser, Farquhar 109
Fraser, George 109
Fraser, Hugh 109
Fry, James 113
Fryer, Trevor 130
Gaban, J 52
Galbraith, Mrs 21
Galer, E 74
Gales, Alfred 47
Gallagher, John 41
Gibbon, D 70
Gibson, H 89
Gibson, James 129
Gilbert, James 116, 119,
129
Gilchrist, Thomas 67
Gill, Frederick 90
Gordon, James 144
Grant, James 114
Gray, Captain W 86
Greathead, Henry 95-6
Grieg, Roy 50
Grey, Captain 25
Grey, George 67
Groat, William 120
Hall, Captain John 34
Hall, Lieutenant Basil 129
Halverson, Yngvar 138
Hamilton, Archibald 121
Ham, J 41
Han, Ab 57
Hardy, Robert 109
Harling, Robert Douglas
52
Harnwell, Robert 59
Harrison, Andrew 116
Harrison, Captain 90
Harrison, Ernest 51-3, 57
Harrison, James 21, 50
Harrison, Ralph 126
Harrison, Richard 126
Harrison, Robert 21

Harrison, Thomas 50
Harrison, William 44-45,
105
Hartland, W 45
Hastings, Francis 21
Hastings, James 58
Hastings, Josh 21
Hastings, M 49
Hakesworth, Mr 72
Hayley, John 31
Hayling, Captain 38
Hefness, Captain Endre 60
Hegeson, John 121
Henderson, Mr 54
Henderson, Mrs 54
Heron, Benjamin 120
Heslop, Thomas 126
Hindley, Job 20
Hitchens, Captain 91
Hodgson, George 19
Hodgson, Jerry 50
Hodgson, John 27
Hodgson, Joseph 92
Hodgson, Robert 21
Hogg, Anthony 126
Hogg, John 130
Hook, W 88
Holden, Isaac 31
Holdsworth, Ian 70
Hood, Charles 25
Hood, Henry 2, 17, 25,
39, 42-45, 67
Hood, Jacob 67
Hood, Robert 17, 24-25,
28, 34, 36-37, 44-45,
58, 63-5, 67, 70
Hood, Thomas 21, 49
Hood, William 17, 23-25,
44-45, 67
Horsley, George 21
Horsley, John 21, 49, 58
Horsley, Robert 58
Horsley, William 21-22, 49
Houghton, Henry 29, 67
Howling, Captain Thomas
111, 114
Hudson, Captain 82
Hunter, Matthew 21
Hunter, Robert 21
Huntridge, W 21
Humphries, Captain 50
Hurdman, William 53
Hutchinson, Mr 109
Ingleby, Charles 16
Jack, Alexander 109-10
Jackson, Alexander 22
James, Andrew 126
Jefferson, HW 70
Jefferson, Thomas 44
Jerningham, Mrs 16
Johansson, OF 50
Johnson, George Moses 89

Johnson, Henry 121
Kare, William 35
Kell, Mr John 37
Kemp, Captain 122
Kemp, James 113
Kendall, J 44, 45
Kennedy, John 21
Kenny, Martin 130
Kirby, George 107
Kirtley, William 30
Kitson, F 44, 45
Kobke, Captain Soren 64
Lake, Captain John 23
Lawlan, Captain A 122
Lawrence, Captain 50
Lawson, Rev John 20, 36, 43, 46
Leeming John 21
Leng, Captain Richard 45
Le Sauvey, Captain 81
Lisle, George 130
Lisle, Mrs Tom 130
Lister, Mr John 36
Lithgo, James 19, 49-50, 56
Lithgo, John 19, 50, 59
Lovibond, George 16
Lucas, Frank 45
Lukin, Lionel 94
Maiden, Robert 70
Marns, William 31
Marshall, John 84, 88, 92
Mason, Walter 49
Massingham, Captain 99
Martin, Captain 118
Mather, Alexander 121
Mattison, Bella 130
Mayors, Henry 27
McLaren, William 121
McKenzie, Peter 109
McKerrell, William 20
McPherson, Donald 52
Mead, David 88
Metcalfe, James 67
Mills, A 52
Mills, Thomas 105
Mitchell, Captain 75
Mole, Kevin 130
Moore, Captain F 41
Morley, Captain George 41
Morrison, Captain John 114
Morse, R 88
Mummin, Sadi 57
Neil, George 88
Nestrom, August 89
Nicholson, George 120
Nilson, Carl 49
Nilsson, Captain 47
Nixon, Anthony 129
Nixon, Mr 89
Nixon, Selby 120
Northumberland, Duke of 97-8
Nugent, Michael 130
O'Conner, Michael 70
Packman, Edward 84
Palmer, Captain 76
Palmer, D 45
Paris, Captain E 122
Park, Captain Peter 80
Parker, John William 55
Parvels, Captain H 99

Patience, Alexander 109
Patience, George 109
Pattison, James 43
Patton, Captain 123
Peake, James 98
Pemberton, RL 89
Perkins, H 45
Peterson, Carl 39
Petersson, Jons 91
Pile, John 111
Pinchin, William 52, 55-6
Pitblado, William 121
Plough, Captain J 123
Plowman, William 90
Plummer, John Henry 30
Pope, Captain J 91
Pottinger, Hugh 30
Pounder, Anthony 21
Pounder, James 21, 49, 58
Pounder, John 21, 58
Pounder, Thomas 21, 67
Pounder, W 49
Price, James 22
Proctor, William 44-45
Prosser, Henry 32
Pullen, Captain HP 85-6
Purvis, Martin 126
Querie, John 121
Quilter, Frederick 88
Randyll, Mr T 22
Ranson 91
Ranson, Captain 84
Redford, John 105, 107, 129
Reed, Thomas 49
Reed, W 88
Reid, Peter 98
Richardson, Captain 34
Richardson, Nathaniel 123
Rievelly, Captain 103
Robinson, Captain 110
Robinson, Captain A 128
Robinson, Joseph 105
Robinson, Richard 23, 50
Robinson, Robert 44-45
Robson, Edward 114
Rodger, Captain 131
Rogers, John 88
Rowntree, Ben 67
Rowntree, Thomas 46, 49, 58
Russ, Captain 76
Rutherford, Robert 130
Sadler, Ralph 52
Sandland, John 144
Schulte, B 49
Scotte, G 46
Scott, Captain James 52-3, 56
Scott, George 88
Scott, John 22, 88
Scott, Morley 88
Scott, Walter 102
Sharp, Sir Cuthbert 22
Sharpe, Captain John 40
Shaw, John Davidson 16
Shepherd, John 21
Sing, Ah 57
Skynner, WH 72
Smeed 119
Smith, Captain Alexander 126

Smith, George 105
Smith, John 105
Smith, Kenneth 130
Smith, Robert 129
Snowdon, Robert 21
Sotheran, J 49
Sotheran, Frank 58, 63, 67
Sotheran, Frank junior 58, 63, 67
Sotheran, G 49
Sotheran, Shepherd 57-8, 68
Sotheran Shepherd junior 58
Spence, John 114
Spence, Joseph 114
Spencely, Captain Francis 26
Stainbridge, Captain Henry 107
Stafford, Joseph 31
Steel, John Richard 45
Stenerson, Captain 110
Stenerson, Captain TS 126
Stewart, Marquis Charles 72
Strachan, Henry 128
Strersen, Theodore 58
Stocks, William 105
Stoker, Thomas 120
Storer, Ambrose 45
Storer, George 50
Storer, Thomas 19
Storey, William 105
Storm, William Pearson 45
Strover, Mary Ann 45
Stupple, Henry 121
Sutton, Henry 30
Svenson, Johan August 61-2
Swain, S 61
Taylor, Andrew 129
Taylor, Barty 105
Taylor, John 105
Taylor, John Henderson 30
Taylor, Robert 105
Thomlinson, Major 54
Thompson, R 92
Thompson, Thomas 105
Thorpe, Thomas 129
Trew, John 22
Tribe, George 55, 57
Tully, John 29
Tully, William 128
Turner, Captain J 125
Urbin, Jean 76
Vart, William 27
Vernon, Arabella 97
Victoria, Queen 42
Vollum, William 22-23
Waddle, John Swallow 120
Wake, Thomas 50
Wallace, D 88
Wallis, James 144
Walton, John 107
Ward, William 76
Watkins, William 31
Watson, Henry 107
Watson, Humphrey 26
Watt, Thomas 21
Webster, J 49, 58
Webster, William

Stephenson 27
Welsh, William 76
Whale, John 126
Wheeler, William 129
Wilkinson, William 22
Willard, Captain William 124
Williams, Captain George 50
Williams, JB 49
Williamson, John 22
Wilson, Henry 86
Woodhave, William 95-6
Woodrow, George 121
Wood, Thomas 120
Young, 91
Young, Gilbert 116
Zeplieu, Captain 25

Sailing Vessels
Adventurer 94
Agamemnon 44
Albatross 77
Albion 122
Alcor 91
Alexander 75
Alliance 34
Alma 103
Alphonse Maria 41
Amelia 24, 38, 40
Amphitrite 103
Amulet 25
Anne 70
Annie Henderson 132
Anns 103
Antelope 103
Apollo 81
Ardwell 113
Arethusa 103
Astley 123
Atlas 42, 67
Aurora 86-9
Awu Maru 51
Ayres 29
Barley Rig 131
Beaver 76
Beeswing 38
Ben Aden 131
Bessheim 130
Betsy 21
Blanche 87
Blenheim 123
Blessing 132
Blossom 81
Blue Fin 130
Border Chieftain 116
Branch 37
Breeze 96
Brilliant 25
British Ensign 84
British Officer 139
British Queen 40
Burnhope 131
Burton 117
Bute 132
Caesar 110
Cairnglen 134-5, 137
Cambois 90-1, 110
Cambria 41
Carmethen Coast 133
Catherine, 68
Catherina 31, 49

Catherine and Mary 125
Catherine Green 79
Challenger 52-3
Champion 55
Chance 28-29
Christina 126
Christine 110
City of Dublin 52
Clara Richmond 37
Claremont 122
Clavering 51-59
Conqueror 84
Conrad 82
Content 78
Constance Ellen 110, 126
Constantia 129
Contractor 25
Coral Queen 40
Cornucopia 49
Corsair 37
Countess of Durham 100
Crathie 131
Cygnet 101
Cyrus 32
Dapper 26
Dauntless 45-46
Devonshire 79
Diamant 118
Don Quixote 81
Doris 63-7, 70
Dorothy 75
Dove 75
Duke 29
Dunhelm 129
Earl Percy 115-6
Economy 67
Edward Cohen 100
Eileen Duncan 137
Eliza 102
Elizabeth 103
Eliza Bain 92
Elizabeth and Sarah 33
Empress 29
Era 29, 67
Eugenia Chandris 139
Euston 132
Eweretta 103
Express 31, 33, 41
Fenella 122
Firelight 133
First of May 122
Florence 49
Flying Huntsman 123
Folkestone 41
Fowlis 107, 109
Francais 38-40
Friends 78
Friendship 77, 111-4, 116,
   128-9
Gaea 131
George Andreas 34
Girl's Friend 131
Good Intent 75, 78
Golden Lilly 126
Granite 44-45
Haldis 58-9
Hannah 103
Hannah and Jane 50
Harmony 81
Harriot 90
Harry Clem 124

Harvest 78
Haslingdean 133
Hawkswood 70
Hebe 38
Helen Cook 78
Helvetia 132
Henry and Elizabeth 86
Henry Cooke 120
Hero 53, 133
Hibbert 29
Hibernia 55
Huntley 86
Hypolite Marie 100
Ida Duncan 132
Ilse 136
Indus 110
Inga 128
Inverlane 133-4
Isabella Miller 37
James 128
James and Ann 103
James Hartley 79
Jane 78
Jane and Elizabeth 100
Jane Green 29-31
Jeanette and Mary 81
Jesse Stevens 20
Johanna 123
John and Amelia 77
John Cock 41
Jonkoping One 133
John Liddle 123
John Miles 133
John Murray 79
Johns 29
Jubilee 28-29
Junius 103
Kate 78
Kelso 35
Kelsey 34
King James 132
Kingston 75
Lady Ann 92
Lalla 31
La Morlaye 130
Lavinia 118
Liberty 35
Lile 91
Lively 100
Louise 25
Lovely Nelly 104, 107
Margaret Caithness 40
Margaretta 129
Maria 34, 78
Marie Elizabeth 99-100
Marquis of Huntley 23
Mary 28
Mary and Jane 78
Mary Ann 78, 83
Mary Clark 78
Mayflower 34
Melancholie 76-7
Messenger 103
Minerva 107
Mirror 32
Miss Thomas 91
Mulgrave 35
Muristan 129
Napoleon 76
Native 29
Nautilus 75

Newark Castle 132
New Cornwall 123
Northam 25
Northsider 130
Nymph 29
Olaf Kyrre 125
Oslofjord 130, 135, 137,
   139
Orbit 32
Orwell 35
Otra 60-62
Peep O Day 132
Percy 129
Pilot 78
Presto 59-60
Primrose 50
Prince 120
Princess 32
Progress 129
Providence 34, 38
Queen of the Isles 84
Queen Victoria 25
Quillota 89
Rebecca and Elizabeth 103
Rebecca Johanna 76
Recepto 133
Regalia 67
Rescue 86
Rheinland 124
Rienzi 81
Rio Colorado 133
Rising Sun 31, 33
Robert and Mary 38
Rohilla 97, 129
Rosa 133
Rosa Glen 54
Rose 37, 82
Rosella 131
Sarah Ann 77, 107
Sarah Helen 103
Savannah 33
Scotia 41
Scylla 118
Seal 131
Seven Sons 122
Snowdrop 82-3
Southsea 139
Spy 35
Sprite 4
Stanley 27, 111-6, 129
St Lawrence 27
Swan 36
Teal 13
Thomas 50
Thomas and Margaret 35
Thomas and Mary 35, 38,
   40
Thomas Clarkson 77
Time 62
Treaty 110
Trio 45-48
Trois Seaurs 81
Tyro 75
Union 29, 100
Unity 99
Vestra 132
Vixen 59
Wansbeck 34
Watchful 132
Wave 82
Wave Queen 50

William and Mary 100
William Crowe 23
William Wake 109, 112
Wonga 123
Woodbine 99
Wrecker 36-37
Young John 68
Zeeland 132
Zeno 41
Zillah 77-8
Zosteria 85-6

Lifeboats
Bradford 20, 72
California 116
Cambois 129
Caroline Clagett 74
Charles Dibden 96, 122
Charles Ingleby 41, 45, 50,
   54-55, 57, 60
Charles Mather 16
Charlotte 18, 20
Constance 96, 116-7
Co-Operator No 1. 96, 98
Cyclist 45, 46, 68
Duke of Wellington 74
Elizabeth Newton 63-7
Elliott Galer 74, 79-80
Florence Nightingale 74
Forester 94, 96, 118, 124
Forester's Pride 16
Francis Whitbourn 19-20
Friend of all Nations 72
Good Templar 74, 83
Henry Vernon 97, 129
Ilminster 49, 55, 58
James Davidson Shaw 16
J McConnell Hussey 97
Job Hindley 20, 39-40
John and Amy 74
John Clay Barlow 16, 41
John Foulston 74
John Lawson 20, 43-4
John Pyemont 138
Junios 74
Mary Isabella 20
Nancy Newbon 74, 87
Northumberland 95-6, 110,
   116, 129
Original 95
Palmerston 120
Percy 105
Prior 96
Providence 95-6, 107-8,
   110, 112, 116
Richard & Nellie Hodges
   74, 85
Rochdale 16
Sisters Carter of
   Harrogate 72, 78, 88
Skynner 70
Spirit of Northumberland
   95
Tees 17, 20, 23, 25, 28
Tom Perry 124, 130
Tyne 95-6, 107-10, 112,
   126, 129
Westmoreland 138
William Hedley 74
Zetland 25